wishes

Adrian

The Ghost Detective series

Ghost Detective I: ISBN 978-0-9532563-3-4

Ghost Detective II: ISBN 978-0-9532563-4-1

Ghost Detective III: ISBN 978-0-9532563-5-8

Ghost Detective IV: ISBN 978-0-9532563-7-2

Ghost Detective V: ISBN 978-0-9532563-8-9

www.ghost-detective.org.uk

©Adrian Perkins 2015

The right of Adrian Perkins to be identified as the author of this work has been asserted in accordance with the Copyrights, Design, and Patent Act. 1988.

All rights reserved. No part of this book may be reprinted or reproduced or utilised in any form or by any electronic mechanical or other means, now known or invented, including photocopying and recording, or in any information storage or retrieval system, without the written permission from the author.

British Library cataloguing, in publication data.

A catalogue record for this series of books is available from the British Library.

Acknowledgements

I would like to thank the following people and organisations for their assistance and patience.

Dawn Branigan, for her hospitality, photos, and history of the **First Light Photographic** property in Daventry.

Ashleigh Fitzhugh, and the team at the **Olde Red Lion** in Kislingbury for their hospitality and patience.

Tim & Roberta Casentieri and **Inchy.**

Michele Perkins, great cover ghost.

To all the eyewitness contributors.

BBC Radio Northampton for their continuing support.

Northampton Records Office.

To the **Tutchener** family for access to information contained in the book, **Kislingbury, a glimpse at its past**.

By **J. V. Tutchener**.

Lewis Dellar.
Diploma with Distinction in Parapsychology Dip...Ppsy.AM.INST.FP
College of management science London.
SCOP HND, Parapsychology.

Pauline Morgan Psychic-Medium

Howard Morgan Locations assistant and photographer.

Mark Thomas, Photographer & Photographic technician.

Book Cover
By
Lisa Walker

Ghost Detective
VI

Written

By

A H Perkins

Copyright © A H Perkins

All rights reserved

Dedicated

To my sons

Adam & David

Who think their dad's a bit weird.

Paris & Wolf Publishing

Northampton

May 2015

ISBN

978-0-9532563-9-6

Introduction

During the investigations and interviews for this book I have met some extremely interesting people. I consider investigating any haunting as a privilege because in most cases you are meeting someone for the first time so they are understandably wary of you. It's up to you to explain what you do and why you do it. Many of the hundreds of people I have helped over the years are now good friends, and without their cooperation these books would never have been written.

Stories of hauntings pop up in the most unlikely places, schools, factories, newly built houses, the list is endless. But by far the most common locations are people's homes. That's why a professional approach should always be foremost in the mind of the investigator.

For me Northamptonshire contains a kaleidoscope of paranormal activity. You have everything on your doorstep that a budding investigator could want. There are huge stately homes with sprawling estates, manor houses, castle ruins, abandoned churches, ancient villages, and battle fields. What more could you want? This county has and will, continue to supply me with investigation material for years to come. Here is a little tip for all you would-be investigators.

Never assume anything, and record everything.

Enjoy.

First Light Photographic

First Light Photographic was established in March 2003 by award winning photographer Dawn Branigan.

The shop and photographic studio is situated on the High Street in the bustling market town of Daventry in Northamptonshire. At first glance the property is just one of a number of retail outlets that line the busy street. But if you delve deeper into its history you will be in for quite a surprise. It is by far one of the oldest properties in the street. During renovation work carried out in 2013 strange things started happening in the shop and photo studio above. So what could have caused such a sudden burst of activity? There had been the odd incident over the years like cold spots in rooms and the sound of someone walking about upstairs. But this new activity was different, and much stronger. While workmen were removing the render from the upper level frontage of the shop a hole in the wall revealed a room in the roof space nobody knew existed. A closer inspection revealed the attic itself had not been entered for many years. Fragments of wallpaper from old panelling in the newly discovered room had newspaper pages used as lining paper stuck to them and the date on the pages read May 1886. There was a bell system fixed to the wall just inside the attic room that seemed to be operated by a wire and pulley system leading downstairs. The room itself was modest in dimensions with plastered ceiling and wallpapered walls, a bedroom perhaps? Another discovery in the attic was that of a child's tricycle. Now remember I mentioned cold spots in a room. The cold spot was directly below where the tricycle was discovered.

Let us now look a little way into the history of the property and see what we can find out. Towards the end of the story I will go into its history in a little more depth.

From the construction of the loft and the exposed beams to the front of the property a date around 1450 has been suggested. To the rear of the property was once an open courtyard and looking up at the building from that point you can see the remains of an old window built from ironstone with mullion supports. I have seen examples of these windows in other buildings which date from the early1500's. Outbuildings have been added on and the original thatch roof of the property now has tiles. Indeed this building shows its age from the many alterations done over the years, each leaving its date by its own particular style. Someone once said, "Archaeology is like peeling back the layers of an onion, peeling back the years to the starting point that is the core.

It would be interesting to see if the buildings to the sides of the photographic shop have a similar structure in the loft space. This would tell us if the building was once a detached property. If you look at the photographs of the loft space you can see this looks probable. As for its first use it is thought the house was originally built as a town house for a family with some influence in the town. Equally it could have been owned by the church as many of the first substantial buildings were.

Above is a photo of the attic at First Light Photographic

The photos below show the front façade when the modern render was removed

A later edition, but ancient nevertheless, the top of an old window frame, again hidden by the render. The half-timbered façade, original beams dating back to the 1450s, hidden by the ugly render until now.

The picture above shows the extra room built into the attic, complete with door, you can also see where a ceiling had been put in from the remnants of lath & plaster attached to the beams. I don't think I would have liked to have slept here as there are no windows.

An old piece of wallpaper, dating back to the 1880s, found in the attic! The colours still show through, as they haven't seen the light of day in 125 years!

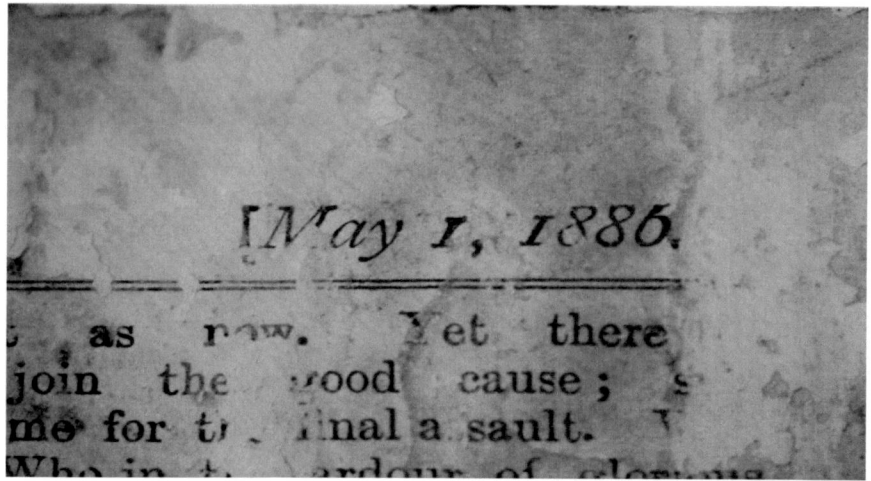

The date of the newspaper used as lining paper before the wallpaper was hung.

A vintage Raleigh tricycle said to have belong to one of our resident spirits. A cold spot in a particular upstairs room had been reported many times. Was it coincidental that the cold spot was directly below where the trike was found in the attic? The Raleigh Bicycle Company was originally based in Nottingham. Founded in 1887 it is one of the oldest bicycle companies in the world. This trike was the pride and joy of a child many years ago. But who was the owner.

Now before I go into the full history of the property let us first go into the investigations regarding its ghosts and where they were located in the shop. Yes I did say ghosts and not ghost. I started this investigation thinking this is going to be simple enough, how wrong could I be?

My initial interviews with Dawn the shop owner, and Mark her assistant proved to be very interesting. Both had a strict religious upbringing. Dawn a strict Methodist upbringing and Mark was brought up in a super strict Christian family. It was interesting to see how this upbringing had caused them both to rebel and to question what they had been told to believe. This questioning was not done in a derisory way but more in an attempt to see if there were other answers to many questions they formed throughout their lives. Two people working together with different personalities, but who through their upbringing have formed a constant thirst for knowledge and a better understanding into the mysteries of life. That is something a blinkered belief system can never achieve. I always do these interviews because I need to get to know the people I am going to be working with, and I need to know how they will interpret any activity that happens. Knowing what they believe helps me understand their interpretation. My plan of action was as follows. Initial walk around with Dawn, Mark, and my parapsychologist friend Lewis Dellar, also medium Pauline Morgan and Pauline's husband Howard would join us. This would be followed up by two investigations, the location of which would be determined by information gathered by Pauline. I always encourage people to speak out and say if they sense anything and this approach has worked well in the past.

The initial walk around was very informative and gave us names and dates to investigate. Added to this the strange sounds I recorded, I considered this a brilliant start. I should just point out at this stage that during this investigation I wore headphones attached to a digital Dictaphone. This helps me in two ways, as well as recording sounds others miss, it can also pick up interference from mobile phone signals. If people are using EMF or K2 meters and I am using the afore mentioned equipment I can instantly tell if the mobile phone signal is affecting the meters. Even GPS on a mobile gives a reading on EMF and K2 meters.

Some weeks prior to this investigation Pauline came to the shop to have some publicity shots done. While being led upstairs to the photo studio she instantly felt a presence. Saying nothing at the time the photo shoot commenced and Pauline became aware there were a number of spirits around them. Dawn's trusted camera battery died quite unexpectedly and the lights were playing up, fluctuating in strength and so on. It was clear from our walk around the construction work being carried out would mean the investigation would be a lengthy one. Normally as work starts the activity starts and again as work concludes so the activity concludes. But in this case work started and stopped midway, to conclude at a later date, so there will be more to come, good or bad. Ok back to the walk around.

As we stood in the photo studio Dawn said she felt as though things had been released suddenly. Lewis asked Dawn if the activity she felt was physical or emotional. Dawn replied it was just a feeling she got, and the unmistakable sense of being watched, nothing physical. She went on to explain that she had noticed customers' dogs taken into the studio always looked up and stared into one corner. She also noticed when young children were having their photos taken they did the same. As Dawn was saying this Pauline said she was aware of a man standing close by who stated they were in his territory and should leave. In her mind's eye she could also picture a Christmas tree by the window and a little girl running around shouting "Daddy's coming home. Daddy's coming home".

As we moved into the corridor on our way to the rear storage room Pauline saw two young men. One of the men was unable to walk without the assistance from the other, as if he was being carried to a doctor for help. Approaching the back storage room Dawn remarked that this was her sanctuary, or her calm room. This part of the building was a relatively new addition. While standing in this room Pauline started picking up on a hospital type room with beds full of sick people, people suffering from a viral infection of some kind. She also felt as though we were in the way of what was going on in there and she began to smell a horrible sulphur type stench. Lewis remarked that this was interesting because people who have had a near death experience have reported smelling a strong sulphurous odour. This smell is also associated with a negative entity, an evil spirit, and one you really do not want to come across.

A strong sense of claustrophobia suddenly seemed to hit Lewis, Pauline, and Howard. This feeling was so powerful we vacated the room and went back into the corridor. I have known Lewis for many years and this was a first, he is usually unaffected by these things. It was Dawn that seemed unaffected on this occasion, probably because, as she said earlier, she treats that room as her sanctuary. An interesting choice of words!

I remarked to Lewis that the floor in the corridor from the back room was uneven and it gave me a feeling of being lifted up. It is strange how uneven floor surfaces can trigger a number of psychological effects, dizziness, and feelings of being physically pushed forward or back.

Walking back along the corridor to our immediate left was a small stock room that Dawn invited us to look at. Now we know this was a modern construction possible only thirty to forty years old but there was something about the room that struck a chord with Pauline and me. Pauline picked up on a tall bossy woman standing as if she disapproved of us being anywhere near her. Pauline also picked up on Salvation Army uniforms. I felt the room was too small and felt as though I wanted to push the walls back. Pauline felt as though there should have been an adjoining door to another room. Dawn was able to verify this was true there had indeed been a door to another room. Pauline also picked up on children and bibles scattered about as though this was once a Sunday school of sorts.

As we moved back into the corridor Pauline said she felt as though a baker had died and been laid out here for a while before being taken out and placed into a horse drawn carriage, the horses wore black plumes; it had been a big occasion with hundreds of people attending. We walked back to the entrance of the studio and Pauline picked up on a large lady who was carrying a big steaming pot and ladle. The woman was shouting in a language Pauline did not recognize, but she seemed to be saying, "Make way, make way". Pauline said it was like the old English style language.

It seems from what people were picking up, this building, certainly in its earlier days, was used for a myriad of functions. We know from the mid 1800's what it was used for, but the earlier years seem very confusing at the moment.

We made our way back down the stairs and decided to check out the main part of the shop before going out to the rear of the property to see if we could get any information from what was out there.

In the main shop there have been some strange mischievous incidents. A shop assistant who was sat at a computer desk had something hit the back of her heel with some force after she had heard something roll across the floor, but they could find nothing. Even when Dawn tried to recreate the incident the floor slopes away from where she was sitting so nothing could have simply rolled toward her, it must have been rolled with force to get to her, a bit like rolling marbles uphill if you like. Dawn said she feels nothing happens at the back of the main shop because this is part of the extension. However, when Pauline and I walked to the rear of the shop you could feel a definite difference between the old and the new buildings. It was like a stomach churning anxiety change from one part of the building to the other. You could draw a line at the very point it changed. I have never come across such a change in atmosphere as strong as this before and I must admit to being a little mystified at that point.

    We decided to go and look at the back yard of the shop to see if this could give us some clues. As you go to walk out of the shop at the rear you pass a cupboard on your left. This is actually the space under the stairs. Dawn said she has had some bizarre things happen close to this spot. When I asked her to explain she said photo frames have flown from the wall, across the shop, and fallen to the floor without breaking, a distance of at least seven or eight feet. Close by this cupboard Pauline picked up on children counting. Mark had also heard a child counting while he was working in the shop. He said it sounded like a child counting at the start of a hide and seek game. Lewis was also picking things up at the same spot. He said he could sense someone signing a large book with an old fountain pen; a land registry book was his first thought. Logical Lewis can be very accurate at times and I have learnt over the years to make a note of what he comes up with.

    Walking out into the courtyard there is a small brick outhouse in front and slightly to your left. The yard is narrow with extensions to the right leading back some ten or so yards. Some of the original extensions further back have been demolished leaving a gap to a small brick built shed at the far end. There are signs of open drainage similar to that found in an animal yard. There is also an entrance to the cellar covered over by a heavy metal lid. Originally this would not have been the main entrance. I believe this was used as utility access for storage or deliveries. The original entrance has been blocked off so this hole in the yard is the only way in today. Dawn pointed out the Tudor stone window high up on the back of the property. Now when you see something like that you know you have a serious building on your hands. Pauline felt the presence of children at play, and said there were cats walking around them, this is something to note for later. Pauline added that one particular girl had walked up to her and offered her a posy of purple violets. Children seem to figure heavily in the activity here.

The small brick built shed at the end of the yard seemed to give everyone the same impression, that of a slaughter house with penned animals. There are open drainage channels running from within the shed so it could be suggestion, but all the same it's worth looking into. Pauline said there should be a well to the side of the shed; she also got the names Alfred or Albert, Rudders or Rutherford. The strongest feeling that Pauline felt that evening was one of protection toward Dawn. It was like she had a caretaker, but not of the property, more one of the soul, a guardian angel if you like. We ended our search of the yard and headed back into the shop to discuss further investigations. I wanted to do two investigations, one upstairs, and one in the cellar. Dates for these would have to be arranged and equipment set up in advance.

When I got home and reviewed the sound recording I had made during the initial walk around I was in for quite a shock, there were other voices on the recording mimicking and generally having fun at what we were saying. We also recorded whistling and a shriek from within the building, but we were the only ones in there. It's strange to hear such recordings back, because we were totally oblivious to the sounds being made. I always record during every investigation I conduct and this happens every single time. I have hours of recordings and always let people hear them if they wish to.

At 10 pm, 25/5/13 the first full investigation began at First Light Photographic. It would be split into two halves, one session in the shop, and one up in the studio. At that time I was being filmed for a documentary about peoples beliefs, so people attending the investigation were Ben from the documentary crew, Dawn, Mark, Lewis, Pauline, Howard, and myself. We began in the studio and I asked each person what their expectations were of the night ahead, I wanted to gauge people's feelings. Lewis said he thought the evening would be more emotional rather than spiritual. He went on to explain that people's expectations of what an investigation was, very often surpasses the reality of what actually happens. TV investigations show spirits around every corner when in truth this is never the case. He added he will be watching how people react to different situations.

I asked Pauline to introduce herself and explain what she does. Pauline is a natural clairvoyant medium and has had the ability to sense spirit from an early age. She had already sensed spirits within the building and said she felt others among the group would also experience similar feelings as the evening progressed.

Then I asked Mark for his expectations for the night ahead. He said that working in the building during the day was normal, but this evening for him was unusual, and very exciting. He added, it would be good to see if the sounds they hear during the day develop into something tangible, something you can recognise as real. I turned to Howard next and asked him the same question. Howard is Pauline's husband and accompanies her on all her events. He said he was going to look closely at all the things people felt tonight and would try to gauge whether their experience is spiritual and not triggered by something natural.

Now for Dawn the owner of the property. She is often there working on till the early hours in the morning and feels as though she is not alone, unseen eyes, and so on. She is apprehensive about the evening's investigation and thinks it will be interesting. I know Dawn has researched the history of the building and she has agreed not to share the information with anyone, including yours truly.

Now for young Ben hiding behind his camera. I wanted him to join in as much as possible into tonight's investigation so I asked him the same question. He said he finds the whole subject very interesting but it got a little scary last time he was filming with us so he asked not to be isolated from the group. He finds the topic a little frightening and would like to remain on the side-lines filming rather than taking part.

Lewis than asked me what I was expecting from tonight. I am intrigued due to the nature of the building and its obvious history. Are the sounds simply echoes from the past, or are there indeed spirits here that can move the trigger objects I have placed here and there. As always I am open to all suggestions, natural or supernatural.

Before we get into it there may be people reading this saying hang on, Lewis is a parapsychologist and Pauline is a clairvoyant medium, they are going to argue and disagree on everything. Not true! Lewis is looking at the mechanics behind how Pauline picks up on spirit. This is not a judgmental thing it's a learning process. And it's the same with Pauline, she knows none of us are there to judge her abilities; it's a learning process for all of us. If you close your mind to the abilities of others you soon become a very lonely and isolated person.

I began the evening's events by asking people to participate in the Extended Memory Recall experiment we have tried in the past. We have fine-tuned the experiment and find it most informative and useful for the participants and ourselves. I asked the group to look around the room for two to three minutes and then we turned the lights out. I then asked them to visualise the room empty of clutter, a bare room. Then they were asked to let their imagination to take over. Allow objects and people into the room and allow this to develop. If there are people, talk to them in their mind, ask questions. If just objects appear then, what are they, do they follow a pattern or theme. Whatever comes in just go with it until I ask you to clear the imagined room and focus back on the group. I will then go round the group asking what they have experienced or seen. In the past there have been people who have seen actual events that we know happened within a property, and there would have been no way they could have known about them.

So what did our group come up with? Mark first. He saw a girl appear in the room with a distinctive cut hairstyle and wearing a pink dress. She dominated his room and he could see nothing else come in. Lewis saw two men wearing long white coats and they had a large old push pull saw. He said he thought the room was bigger than its present dimensions and he also saw a little boy stood in the corner dressed in stereotypical Victorian clothing, short breeches, white socks, black shoes, black waistcoat, white shirt, and a cap. The little boy turned to face the corner as if being punished. Lewis could see the boy sobbing and got the name, Jeffery Gilligan. He seems to think the boy was being punished for taking something he shouldn't have, a bread roll. Lewis then spoke of the men with the saw and thinks they were cutting meat but couldn't see it clearly. Pauline got a man standing to her left with the first name John. He seemed to want to talk to her but before he could a woman appeared to her right waving and playing a tambourine singing a type of Salvation Army song. The woman spoke to Pauline and said she had to be careful of the uniforms. Pauline asked where she kept the uniforms and the woman replied outside in the hallway on shelves. Then Pauline said John wanted to talk to her about his family but the woman's energy standing to Pauline's right was much stronger and the man just faded away. The woman said she had to be quick because they had just had a new intake. Pauline said that's when she heard my voice say, "Start coming back into the room" and the vision faded from view.

Howard was next to say what he saw. Now I had a conversation with Howard earlier about motorbikes. We both love and have ridden bikes for years and it seems Howard unconsciously tuned into that thought and visualised both old and new bikes scattered about the room. This can happen some times, we have a conversation we are really interested in and this conversation is played out again as we relax and allow our thoughts to wander.

Now for Dawn's memory recall. The first image Dawn saw was that of a monk in brown robes seated at a table reading a huge bible. As she looked around the room one image faded and another took its place. To the far end of the room she saw a big wooden table with a woman working at it wearing a black dress, white apron, and mop cap. Then she saw the little boy known as Tom, thought to be the owner of the trike. He had dark curly hair, white shirt, and black braces. At no time was there any conversation with the people she saw.

Now I knew exactly where people were with their thoughts it was time to allow them to explore the property, and their abilities. I know we said we would not go down the cellar until the next visit but it was clear everyone wanted just to have a quick look around. It took a while to get everyone down the ladder but eventually we got in there. The cellar under the shop was quite large with rooms leading off at the end of a long corridor. Pauline instantly got the name Arthur. I know Dawn believes the cellars to be a later addition to the property but if you think about it you would not excavate under an existing building. I believe the cellar directly below the property is older than the extensions leading from it and that the cellar was constructed first and the house was built above with its foundations resting on the arch pillar supports in the cellar. With this in mind, was the property purpose built as a business with storage facilities below? The original staircase leading down into the cellar used to come up in the alleyway to the side of the building.

Anyway back to the group in the cellar. I'm not sure if Mark volunteered, or was persuaded to have a go at the isolation test in the cellar, but praise where praise is due. For someone who, on his first investigation, and who openly admits he is afraid of the dark, to have a go at this shows nerve. After lots of flash photos and a good rummage about we settled Mark down by telling him the walls in some cellars concealed voids in which bodies were hidden never to be seen again. That seemed to cheer him up no end! And for those reading, this is the best way to rid yourself from fear is to meet it head on. Lewis asked Mark to select a room to sit in. Lewis then went back to the entrance in case Mark needed his help or he needed to exit fast.

Above photo shows the entrance to the cellar at
First Light Photographic

Mark was carrying a voice recorder and was asked to record his experiences. The remaining group went back up into the shop but paused at the cupboard under the stairs. Howard got the strangest feeling as he walked by the cupboard. The feeling was so strong that Pauline suggested he sit there for a while to see what happened. I was recording all this and Howard was convinced there was a man who wanted him to leave. "He doesn't want me in here" he said. The instant Howard said in here I picked up a strong male voice saying in an assertive manner, "In here". It sounded to me like a head master addressing a pupil. To my utter astonishment there was no recognition on anyone's face, they had not heard the voice. When I played the recording back people were amazed. Pauline wanted Howard to really concentrate on the man to see if he could glean any information from him. The spirit seemed to think we were there to make fun of him and he wanted us to leave. We thought it best to leave that particular spirit in peace and we walked into the main part of the shop. Pauline started picking up on ladies with large bonnets on their heads and a general business about them. This made perfect sense when you know what this place was, but more on that later.

We made our way back up into the photo studio and settled ourselves down to send thoughts down to Mark, he had been asked to direct thoughts up to us after relaxing for a period of time. Concentration is the key to this and to be honest the noise coming from the road outside was making this extremely difficult. It was also getting extremely cold which did not help matters. We started sending thoughts to Mark and hopefully things would start to happen to him. Pauline said she was seeing the little girl Mark had described and her name was Rosie, but Pauline said the little girl kept pulling her toward the door saying "Go get Mark, go get Mark, we have to get him out". Prior to that Pauline saw a large jolly man by the name of John saying "Boy down stairs", presumably Mark. But the man said it as if it were a secret to be kept. Then the woman Pauline had seen in the experiment earlier came into view, the Salvation Army woman. She was angry and said, "No, he is not welcome up here until he redeems himself, he is not fit to be among us". When Pauline tried to visualise Mark in the cellar, she said although you could tell it was him, the clothes he wore were of a different period in time. It was like he had taken the place of someone else. She also felt as though Mark was feeling as though he was overcoming something, a feeling of empowerment. As Pauline finished explaining what she had seen I suddenly had a picture flash across my mind. I could see Lewis crouching down at the entrance to the cellar, and next to him knelt a little boy in quite ragged clothing with a dirty little cap on his head. He kept looking up at Lewis and then down into the cellar as if to ask, what are you looking at? The frowned expression on the boy's face gave me a strange sick feeling in my stomach as if we should know something or he was trying to tell us something. What Howard said next sent chills down my spine. When he was trying to connect with Mark he could see a little boy at the entrance to the cellar on the trike and another standing with him. The little boy got off the trike and looked down the hole and his taller friend said, "Go on, you go down there". The little one replied, "No, I'm not going down there". The taller of the two then told the little boy to watch him, and he went down some steps into the hole and came back out again saying, "There see I told you it was safe". The little boy then leant over the hole to look down and the taller one pushed him in. There was a cry then silence, and then the taller boy closed the cover to the cellar. Howard said the picture then changes and he could see two people at the entrance to the cellar and one said to the other, "You feed him this time" then the picture faded. Dawn said she had a medium in some weeks before and she had said the medium picked up on a little boy and he goes down into the cellar, that's his place. She said there had been an accident but it wasn't really an accident the boy was pushed.

We could hardly wait to see what Mark was sensing. On his return you could sense the excitement in both him and Lewis. Lewis said when he went to fetch Mark, Mark wanted to stay there. Mark explained that he was sitting down and the first thing he had to do was try to get over his fear of being in the dark but he found that closing his eyes made him feel better and more secure. At first he said he could hear us walking about upstairs and that it seemed ages before things became quiet, only then did he sense something, or someone, was with him. In his mind's eye he could see a small bald man in front of him and he was being aggressive towards him and kept charging at him trying to force him out. Mark kept his eyes tight shut but said he felt as though the man was standing over him, standing by his knee really leaning over him. He asked the man to let Pauline know he was with him and that Mark was afraid. Mark was looking for support at this point. He then began to analyse his situation and said to himself, this is ridiculous, I am on my own in a cellar and there is nothing with me. If you really are here make a sign. Instantly a rock fell to the ground in front of him. Opening his eyes he could see nothing but then he heard footsteps and the shuffling of feet in the long passage that leads to the room where he was sitting. At first he thought it was Lewis because he thought Lewis was in the cellar and did not leave. He had been hearing what he thought was Lewis in the next room all the time he had been down there, but it did not freak him out because he thought Lewis was there. But Lewis had not moved from his position outside at the top of the entrance in the yard.

Mark, still unaware he was totally alone began to see the man again and felt the man's extreme aggression. This chap wanted him out and right now. Mark wanted to confront the chap but did not want to do it alone so he went to get Lewis. His surprise when he shouted to find Lewis was not in the cellar sent a chill down his spine. Mark went to the entrance and asked Lewis to join him. Lewis thought Mark wanted out, but no, he wanted to go back and confront the spirit. With backup Mark was empowered to give some aggression back and Lewis said if the chap is in your face tell him to go, which he did. Mark was now the aggressor and the tables were turned and the spirit left immediately. Lewis and Mark decided to leave the cellar thinking they would join us upstairs but Mark changed his mind on the way back and wanted to go back down, much to Lewis's surprise. Back in the cellar both Lewis and Mark could feel a presence of someone in there running around. There was also a white light flashing which they both saw. It seemed to be associated with Mark and they both describe the light as a soft light moving about. Lewis thought it was actually on Mark at one point. Mark said, yes he could actually see his hands from the brightness of the little light. Mark also saw a blue light go across in front of Lewis.

On their return to the group their report had several similarities to what Pauline said she had been feeling. Pauline was sensing Mark was feeling empowered and Mark confirmed this in his report. I think the feelings he was experiencing came through to her but he was preoccupied with what was happening to him to pick up on what we were sending down to him. For me this experiment touched very tentatively on the abilities I believe our minds have to communicate with each other, in the same way twins are connected, a form of telepathy if you like.

The evening was progressing quite well and I wanted to see who would volunteer to do the emotion test. I explained to the group that this test was not one to go into lightly. It is an extremely difficult task to do and I only wanted someone who was prepared to do the test with one hundred percent commitment. After discussions Mark thought he had the right frame of mind to give it a real go.

I have explained the test before but for those of you not acquainted with this experiment here is how it is done. Set up in a room within this building stands a pendulum suspended with its tip just touching a flat bed of sand. The sand is so fine the slightest movement from the pendulum will result in a line being drawn in the sand. A video camera then records any movement of the pendulum. We first ask the volunteer to go and have a look at the pendulum. On their return I ask them to go through three emotions, anger, sadness, and finally joy. The first two emotions can be swapped about if the person wishes but they must finish on joy. If not you could ruin someone's entire nights experience and that is not the aim. As the volunteer goes into each emotion they are asked to focus the energy towards the pendulum with their mind. The objective is to move the pendulum with emotional energy. I time each of the three emotions to see which, if any emotion moves the pendulum. In the past we have had some successes and it seems women are better at focusing emotion than men. However, this experiment is done to show people that in some cases, when a poltergeist is being blamed for the activity within a property, for example the movement of objects, sometimes it is a person within the building who is unconsciously causing the phenomena rather than a spirit. Eliminate the natural before you blame the supernatural! On this occasion however Mark's result was compromised by a loose floorboard that moved the pendulum as we walked about, shame really but that's how it goes sometimes.

We had been going for about four hours and the cold was starting to set into each and every one of us. Fatigue was starting to show on people's faces and concentration levels were starting to suffer. Remember, upstairs this building had no front wall, just tarpaulin covering the beams so the wind and cold was getting in. Pauline was giving it one last go trying to see if the spirits would make themselves known, while the rest of us were breaking down camera setups and reeling in cables. Packing things away is a tedious job but one that has to be done on each and every investigation. Then quite without warning while I stood with Pauline and Howard in the small room to the rear of the property a loud growling noise was heard. At first I thought it was Lewis fooling about in the yard below us, but when we looked they were still in the cellar putting the equipment away. Then the growl came again, a little louder this time but unmistakably a growl. Then movement was heard about four feet from us, like a shuffling sound. Now remember I told you Marks pendulum test was compromised because of a rickety floor board. When we checked the pendulum again the sand was perfectly smooth, not a line or mark to be seen, how on earth could that be possible. Maybe a spirit with a sense of humour? We ended the night on a high point and decided because of the interference from the road outside the next investigation would be held in the cellar.

On 16/11/13 at 5.30pm The Cellar investigation would start. But first Lewis and I would spend two hours setting up infra-red cameras and laptops to record every movement and sound down there. Not an easy job in the semi dark conditions.

In the picture above you can just make out the ladder used to get down into the cellar. This is the first room you come into and the corridor to the left leads into more rooms beyond.

Picture above shows the middle chamber. Note the wall on the right is of much older construction than the arch roof and wall to the left. We used this room as base of operations.

The end chamber showing a smaller room at one end.

The small room to the side of the end chamber, with new brick built columns supporting the upper floor. Notice the interesting arch in the wall to the left.

The end chamber was once the entrance room as the original staircase shows. Well-worn steps leading down from the street show years of traffic.

As you can see from the photos this cellar is an intriguing place. Blocked archways tell of a time long ago when the rooms went much further under adjoining properties. Sadly many tunnels that once existed along bustling streets have now been separated into individual cellars. This holds true for many towns big or small. So what can we glean from first impressions. An old staircase tells us the cellar once has an entrance situated towards the front of the shop via an alleyway to the side. Some of the partition walls to rooms have old stonework bases and newer brickwork above, and some have new brickwork from the floor to ceiling. This leads me to believe the layout we see today has more rooms than were previously intended. In fact walls in the cellar that are built entirely of stone seem to form the outer foundations of the building above. This being the case I think the cellar was created when the building was first erected. Over time people have added rooms with the new materials.

You may be thinking what is the relevance of this? Well if we know what a cellar once looked like we can then form ideas to its use, and from that an idea of what the property above was used for in its early days. I will give you an example. Say you enter a house and go down to the cellar. You see a gutter running down the centre of the floor leading to a drain. There is a sloping shoot set in the front wall. On the floor adjoining a side wall you see a series of small brick built walls two feet high jutting out. Although you entered a house you are standing in the cellar of a pub, so the building was once a pub. If you are looking for a ghost in a property you must first find out all you can about the building, and in turn the type of people who lived there. At First Light Photographic we have an idea about the cellar but for now let us see what the ghosts and spirits have to tell us down there.

We have heard Mark's previous experience in the cellar and I was eager to see if this experience would have an effect on other members of the group on this occasion. Hopefully it will be on their mind and their senses will be alert for anything out of the ordinary. People attending this investigation were Dawn, Sally, Mark, Pauline, Howard, Lewis, Tina, and me. We had audio and infrared video running at all times and I began by asking people to take a little time to settle down and get accustomed to their surroundings. We each had a chair to sit in and relax. I wanted the group to be as comfortable as possible. From the start we had uplighters illuminating each room and corridor. In fact it was quite cosy down there. An added bonus was the silence and lack of distracting noise from outside. As we settled Pauline became aware of a woman standing close to us holding out a loaf of bread and asking Pauline to try it. The woman was accompanied by a man in a trilby hat and overcoat. Pauline sensed a bad atmosphere around this individual and felt the cellar was once used as a secret meeting place used to inflict punishment on people, away from prying eyes. Interestingly at that moment a small boy appeared to Pauline and said, "That's it Mrs tell it as it is". Pauline had the impression he wanted his story told. The boy faded from view and was replaced with a little girl by the name of Rosie. Rosie was looking at Mark's shoes and was intrigued by them. Apparently she had been following Mark around for a few days since she saw him in the cellar the first time. Mark visibly shivered a little at this news. Pauline explained that the woman that was in the cellar with them was not the same one that had said Mark was not worthy to be in the house. The one now standing in the cellar seems to be a baker of bread and cakes. Pauline formed the impression this woman was down here to try to get someone to eat, or to bring them food. Tina asked Pauline if she could date the woman by what she was wearing. Pauline placed the woman, the little girl, and the little boy, in the late Victorian age. The gentleman in the trilby and overcoat she placed in the nineteen twenties or thirties. Lewis asked Pauline if she thought the bread for the shop was made upstairs and brought down into the cellar to be stored or made down here and taken upstairs. She thought there was a larger oven down in the cellar and a smaller one upstairs. Interestingly while we were setting the equipment up earlier that evening Lewis said he thought a feature in a wall in the cellar looked like an oven. Pauline was picking up the feeling that the baker woman was dominated by her husband. She was a churchgoer but her husband was not, and in public, while out together she smiled, but at home she had to mind her step. Pauline put the woman's age about thirty or forty and her name was Elizabeth. At this point I became aware of light fluctuations and asked Lewis if he could see anything on the monitor that might be the cause, but there was nothing. There was a sudden drop in temperature in the room where the majority of us were sitting. Lewis was still in the adjoining room watching the cameras. Pauline was still getting information from the baker woman and it seems while the woman's husband went to the local marketplace she would hand out bread to, what she described as

"Street urchins". While Pauline was linked with this woman she sensed the woman was glad to be able to express her views on people she could never have done while alive. Her views on the vicar at the time were, should we say less than charitable.

At this point I wanted the rest of the group to try to pick up on anything they could. Everyone has the ability they just rarely get the chance to try it. Lewis suddenly came up with the name Alison Wetherall, and the feeling she was in a wheelchair. We then heard a stone being thrown in a room to our right. For your reference it's the room in the photos with the two modern brick pillars. It was clear on the cameras that we all turned our heads at the same time the sound was heard. Activity was now starting to build and I wanted to keep the momentum up and increase the energy levels people were putting out. Howard then came out with a sentence that at first seemed to make little senses to any of us, "Where should I put the horse so it can't be seen?" Now, I recall sifting through the county court records and seeing that a previous owner of this property was accused of stealing a horse from a neighbouring farm. The records did not give a judgment on the case. Was this a coincidence? I doubt that. Howard also said the name of the horse was Black Bob and that it was blind in one eye. Things were getting interesting!

After a silent time of concentrated awareness the group were firing on all cylinders and we started making progress on names and individuals. Pauline asked Mark if he had sensed a person close to him within the last ten minutes, his reply was, "Yes, how did you know that". Pauline said that she had sensed Rosie was close to Mark and that she had bought a spinning top down to show him. She wanted Mark to be her big brother and she wanted Pauline to be her auntie because she felt secure when she was with them. When Mark had sensed the presence of the girl earlier he had asked her to go to speak to Pauline. Mark wanted to see if he could get closer to Rosie but he did not know how to do it. Pauline suggested he do what I had explained earlier and simply close his eyes, relax, and allow Rosie into his mind. I then explained to the group that to do this successfully you need to blank out all around you and to leave the place you are in and enter an altered state of consciousness. It sounds complicated but we all do it every night when we fall asleep. It's at the point when our conscious mind meets the unconscious. I have seen people actually fall asleep trying to do this. Practise and you will find it actually works. Pauline asked if there was someone in the group who suffered from nosebleeds because Rosie had picked up on this. She also felt the woman sitting next to Dawn should smile more and she was going to fetch her rag doll for her. Dawn then asked Pauline if Rosie had passed over when she was a child or had she become an adult. Pauline replied that Rosie had not become an old lady. Dawn had asked this because we had found a Rosie associated to the property but she was alive into her twenties. Could she be our Rosie? I am often asked about ghosts being seen in their prime by people within their family. We all tend to see ghosts as we would like to remember them. As for someone we have never met it is how the spirit would like to be seen by the viewer that is the answer. Lewis was still watching the monitors and saw a shadow move quickly behind my right shoulder. Tina asked Pauline if the tricycle was Rosie's. Pauline said it was but she had to share it with Tom. Mark then asked a question that only few people knew the answer to. He asked, "What was the original colour of the tricycle"? Pauline asked Rosie and the answer came back, red and blue. Now was this was correct? Yes it was! The trike had been painted over but on investigation the original was indeed red and blue.

While all this information was being recorded I was also recording for EVP's or, Electronic Voice Phenomena. My research has shown on many occasions E.V.P's happen while people are in conversation. The vibration from their voices seems to release other sounds. Often these sounds go unnoticed, or for some scientific reason we are unable to hear them as they are produced. This investigation was no different to others and E.V.P's were being captured, even if we had not noticed them. On several occasions while Pauline was explaining what she was picking up, the digital recorders recorded the sound of a cat or kitten meowing close to us. This sound would have more meaning as the investigation continued.

Pauline then explained that she felt as though the cellar was also used for the sale of black market goods. Tina asked when? Pauline thought it was during the late thirties and into the forties and the sale of nylons was one of the goods on offer. People within our assembled group started feeling something was moving around us going from one person to the next, it seemed as if they were listening to each of us. The little girl Rosie seemed to be with us for the whole of our stay and she wanted us to play games with her. Pauline said Rosie had a giving nature and wanted to make people smile and laugh, basically to cheer them up. Rosie could not understand why we were all wearing different footwear. She also said we all smelt different and did not smell of lavender. Rosie then said she was being called so would have to go, but she would leave the cat with us, she would leave the cat! Remember the E.V.P's? It was not until I played the recording back several hours later that the cat was heard. Nobody in the cellar had heard it. Only Rosie knew it was there.

I decided to switch off lights and carry on the investigation in total darkness, thus taking away the comfort zone people had from lights being on. I started by inviting the spirits Pauline was picking up on to come close to us and to make themselves known. After a short time people started to hear the footsteps of people outside walking along the pavement. This shows how people's senses alter to compensate when it is dark and quiet. The footsteps had been there all the time. I started to see movement behind Pauline, like a dark mass, but I was aware that there was still a light source coming from something. Lewis said the only light still on was the power light on the DVR. This shows how your eyes compensate even with the smallest of lights.

As for the movement I had seen? Pauline described the feeling of someone standing behind her and she felt someone gently pulling her ponytail. Was it a spirit, or shadow I saw? To eliminate this question all light must be off. But we needed the DVR to record the session. Lewis put a piece of cloth over the light and this cured the problem, he then came and sat in the doorway with his back to the outer room. He said he began to feel unprotected from anything in the room behind him. Again this is, as Lewis himself pointed out, a psychological response to being in the dark.

We all naturally feel safe in the dark if we have our back to something, a tree, or wall, it's a primeval defence mechanism we still have. Dawn also explained she had deliberately sat with the wall behind her and not in front of the old staircase because of that very reason. Our fear of the unknown is as relevant today as it was in the past, even though we like to think we are more advanced than our ancestors. However, Pauline did have her back to a wall so what she felt was not brought on by the fear.

We then started to discuss why Mark could not replicate the feelings he had had on the previous investigation. The consensus was because there were more people with him he felt protected. He said even if he were sat in the cellar alone he thought it would not hold the same fear for him as before. Familiarity of a situation brings its own rationality.

After a while even in total darkness I began to see things that I thought unusual. A sudden flash of light high in a corner, curiously not seen by the others, and dark shapes moving between the assembled group. Lewis also started to see movement in the room. Then Mark saw a light flash in a similar location to the one I had seen earlier. Lewis explained to the group that as we were sat in a room bathed in infrared light from the cameras, it is possible we were picking up this light in our peripheral vision. Pauline said that while Lewis was talking someone was patting her knee and saying to her "It's alright darling, it's alright you will get used to it". She said she felt as though the person talking to her was explaining getting use to bombing rather than the lack of light, and they were in an air raid shelter. Interestingly I know buildings around here did use their cellars for air raid shelters during the Second World War. Again Pauline was getting links to black market goods being stored in the cellar. This is extremely possible within a small town during the war.

Lewis suddenly heard a noise, and on turning round thought he saw a flashlight in the cellar tunnel so quickly he went off to investigate. Finding nobody there he returned to the group and as he did so Pauline received the name Jack Cooper, with a military connection to the Air Force, American air force navigator on a B17. I always search the records when given first and last names during investigations, but up to now I can't trace this name in relation to the building. But as I have said many times, the names Pauline comes out with are not necessarily connected to the building the investigation is held in, they may be connected to a person within the group doing the investigation. That's why I always urge people going on investigations like this to shout out the minute they recognise a name or place.

I tried to encourage people in the group to ask out, "If there are any spirits here", and so on. Believe it or not it helps people relax when they do this. I didn't have to ask twice, they all had a go. The increase in the group's enthusiasm had the desired effect. Pauline and several others simultaneously heard movement in the small room behind Howard. Pauline also noticed a shadow movement behind Lewis and a flickering spot of light by his neck and upper chest. Then Mark saw the figure behind Lewis move slightly to the right. After a pause of several minutes Pauline began to receive names relating to the Knightley family. They were a powerful family with their main house at Fawsley and they also had several other town houses in Daventry and surrounding district. The information Pauline was getting seemed to be from the Knightley's tenants and workers complaining about them. It's not surprising really; we all like to have a moan about the boss from time to time. Back then things for the peasant workers were far from idyllic. At this point in the recording the sound of a crow squawking loudly was picked up but astonishingly nobody in the room heard a thing or even gave the slightest reaction. Interestingly part of the Knightley coat of arms at the family church has three ravens on one part of shield.

The cellar investigation drew to a close and with it the paranormal side to the investigation was concluded. The investigation would now turn to the history of the building.

We believe this building is much older than previously thought and could possibly be one of the oldest standing buildings in Daventry. Clues to its alterations over centuries are visible if you look closely. It was Dawn, the owner, who first saw the buildings true potential. Even before it had the modern cladding removed to fix water damage to the front elevation she could see signs that this building was a little special.

The front façade and roof timbers scream of Tudor construction. Houses from this time were mainly made of wood and are sometimes called 'half-timber' houses because they were timber frames filled in with wattle and daub (a mix of interwoven branches, the wattle, and mud, the daub), mortar, brick, or some other fill with a lower section made from stone or brick. If you look back to the photos earlier you will also see the remnants of later lathe and plaster. At a later date the gaps between the beams on Dawn's building were filled in with old window frames and covered in this lath and plaster coating, possibly whitewashed. Even more interesting is the rear of the property where the walls are of a sandstone construction, and just below the guttering is a walled up stone mullion window frame. Fashions of architectural design changed as much back then as they do today, with little regard for what went before.

It is thought the house was first built as a townhouse for a wealthy merchant. It's possible that later the clergy may have owned the property and would have taken rent for it. The first names that are linked to the building come with the Census records. Dawn has traced it back as far as 1836, when Leigh's Bakery was founded by

John Leigh. Below are the census records for people living, working, and boarding at the premises.

1841	Name	Age	
	John Leigh	40	Baker
	Ann Leigh	36	Wife
	Sarah Leigh	3	Sarah died at the age of five after being ill for just 24 hours.
	Rebecca Leigh	1 Day	
	Elizabeth Eales	55	Nurse
	Mary Farey	20	House Servant
	George Orbon	20	Bakers Apprentice
	Thomas Buttin	14	Bakers Apprentice

1851	Name	Age	
	John Leigh	50	Master Baker
	Ann Leigh	45	Wife
	Rebecca Leigh	9	Daughter
	Samuel George Leigh	7	Son
	Ann Leigh	4	Daughter
	Samuel Atkins	23	Baker
	Ann Brown	18	House servant

1861	Name	Age	
	John Leigh	60	Master baker employing 1 man
	Ann Leigh	56	Wife
	Rebecca Leigh	19	Daughter
	Samuel G Leigh	17	Son
	Annie Leigh	14	Daughter
	Edwin Pratt	21	Baker

1871	**Name**	**Age**	
	John Leigh	70	Baker
	Charlotte Leigh	58	Wife
	Rebecca Leigh	29	
	Samuel G Leigh	27	Baker
	Robert Marks	18	Baker

1881	**Name**	**Age**	
	John Leigh	80	Master baker employing 1 man & 1 boy.
	Charlotte Leigh	63	Wife
	Rebecca Leigh	39	
	Saml.Geo. Leigh	37	Baker
	George Haynes	20	Baker
	John Furl	16	Bakers apprentice

1891	**Name**	**Age**	
	Samuel George Leigh	47	Baker
	Sophia Leigh	31	Wife
	John George Leigh	6	Son
	Ann Leigh	5	Daughter
	Mary Eliza Leigh	4	Daughter
	Rose Sophia Leigh	3	Daughter
	Samuel Geo Leigh	7/12	Son
	Austen Hopcraft	17	Bakers assistant.
	Herbert Wiltshire	15	Bakers assistant.
	Marry Burrows	20	Shop woman
	Ann Wilson	20	General servant
	Ann David	14	Nurse

The family then ran the bakery from numbers 3 & 5 High Street in Daventry. They also took on borders.

1901 **Name** **Age**
Samuel George Leigh   57 Baker & Confectioner
employing 4 people
John George Leigh   16 Bread Maker
Ann Rebecca Leigh   15
Mary Elizabeth Leigh 14
Rose Sophia Leigh   13
Samuel George Leigh   10
Lousia Annie Lill   36 Housekeepre
Ann Elizabeth Staley 25 Baker Confectioner
William Foyle   25 Baker
Archibald Frederick Forsman 17 Bakers apprentice.
Ernest Taylor   28 Assistant Schoolmaster
Elizabeth Checkley   16 General servant.

Here is an interesting fact for you to note. Samuel is now widowed and states in the 1911 census the property covers numbers 3 & 5 High Street, where he runs the Temperance Hotel & Restaurant as well as being a baker, pastry cook, & confectioner.

1911 **Name** **Age**
Samuel George Leigh   67 Baker, Pastry Cook, & Confectioner
John George Leigh   26 Working in confectionery,
& Bookkeeping
Mary Elizabeth Leigh 24 Home Keeper
Rose Sophia Leigh   23 Manageress of shop
Frederick Cyril Green 19 Apprentice Confectioner and Draper.

Samuel George Leigh carried the baking tradition well into the 20th Century. He appears in the 1914 census with a bakery at 3 & 5 the High Street. Samuel died on the 1st of April 1922 at the age of 78.
The 1940's Kelly's directory states that at number 5 High Street stood the Leigh's Temperance Hotel. While at number 3 High Street was Mrs E A Leigh's Specialist bakery, specialising in wedding

cakes. When the Leigh's bakery eventually closed, John Harris Leech opened The Danetre Fancy Bakery, at 2-3 High Street in Daventry. According to the deeds, there may have been shoe menders there for a while in the 1950s. Buzzards Electrical were there for a while in the 1960s - I believe they also had a branch in Banbury. In 1967 or thereabouts Geoffrey Creighton took over and Creighton's remained a fixture of the High Street until January 2003, when First Light Photographic opened its doors.

As usual I have tried to match names to known paranormal events recorded over the years, but the research has thrown up a few more questions. The child, Rosie, picked up during the investigation could have well been Samuel's daughter, but we know she lived well into adulthood. Samuel did lose a daughter but her name was Sarah.

Now remember the Pauline the medium picked up on Salvation Army uniforms. The print on the back of the wallpaper used as lining paper in the attic was found to be pages from the War Cry the Salvation Army magazine. Links with the Knightley family are extremely possible, and I would not be surprised if the Knightley family owned several major properties within Daventry during the 15th, 16th, and 17th century. Property and land was the key to prosperity. With land came tenant farmers and rent for their fields and houses. Hand on heart, the history research for this property has been hard going but I hope you will find the information helpful should you wish to research it further.

Is First Light Photographic haunted? Yes

Eyewitness accounts of ghosts

During my travels to festivals and talks I meet a vast number of people who have eyewitness accounts of ghost sightings and other strange events. I thought I would share a few of them with you between investigations. I hope it will show how varied ghost sightings can be.

The Grey Lady of Cranford

The witness to this event was Paul Buttler from Bewdley in Worcestershire. One night while minicab driving from Heathrow at about 4 in the morning he was driving up the M4, turning left down to the parkway takes you by Cranford, with Cranford Park on your right. This was once known as Barkley Manor, the church reputedly being over one thousand years old. As Paul turned left to come down the dual carriageway he suddenly had to brake hard, he could see someone in the road. He described the figure as a woman gliding slowly across the road in front of him. She was dressed in grey and her head, hands, and feet seem to hang limp as she glided along. Paul believes it took the lady a good five minutes to go across the road. Then something caught his eye just for a fleeting moment and looking back the lady had gone. He said at the time he was tired but relaxed and not thinking of anything in particular, he certainly was not expecting to see that. When he returned to the depot surprisingly he didn't get the mickey taken out of him. He was told to speak to Bill in the morning. Bill had worked for the firm for many years so would know the route Paul had driven. In the morning Paul related the story to Bill and described exactly what he had seen. Bill told him he had seen the grey lady of Cranford, and she had been seen many times by other drivers, including Bill. The story Bill told to Paul was, it is believed the woman had lost her children and they had drowned in the river Crane that runs through the park. She constantly searches for them out of guilt and remorse. Bill then asked Paul if he had had a recent bereavement. In fact Paul had just lost his five year old daughter who suffered from Spina Bifida, and died through contracting meningitis, she is buried in that churchyard at Cranford. Bill said it was probably a sign to say she is ok and being looked over by the lady.

Many years later Bill had another daughter who had a strawberry birthmark behind her ear. It matched exactly the spot where his late daughter had had a valve implanted behind her ear as she developed Hydrocephalus or 'water on the brain'. Was this a coincidence? To Paul no! I agree totally, and what a comfort to have.

Thank you for your story Paul.

James Cagney

Here is a story of a strange event told to me by Jo Tarbuck.

In the early hours of the 30th of March 1986 Jo had a very strange dream. A dream that stuck in her mind so clearly it was as though it had actually happened. When she awoke she did not tell her husband at first but waited until they were driving to work down in London. She told him she had had the weirdest dream last night. I dreamt about James Cagney. He was at an airport; Jo went up to him and said "You're James Cagney". "Yes" he replied. Jo then asked him, "Where are you going" and he replied, "I don't know". Jo then said "What do you mean you don't know". His reply was strange, "I have my suitcase and I am going somewhere, but I don't know where I'm going to". Jo said to him "How weird". "Yes, I don't know where I am going at all." he replied. He then walked off and the dream ended. After Jo told her husband he just said, that is weird. Anyway later that day Jo was at work and her husband phoned her and said are you sitting down. "Why", Jo asked. Well it has just been announced on the radio that James Cagney died last night. Was this a coincidence? Jo does not think so, and neither do I.

Story of the Wood Cutter

This story was told to me by Bob Lovell, a local man with a story about his cousin who is a woodcutter.

Bob's cousin had been cutting wood with workmates in a local location for about three days. Late in the evening of the third day they had finished and were sitting around the tractor chatting about what they would be doing the next day. On looking across the field they saw an old fella in a black suit, bowler hat, and with a walking stick walking across the field. Thinking it a little strange one turned to the other and asked, "What's that all about"? With shrugging of the shoulders it was forgotten and they thought no more about the incident. However, the following day they went to the house where the gentleman they had all seen the previous day had been heading. They said to the owner, "Saw something strange yesterday, an old man was walking across the field heading toward your house". The owner asked if the man was dressed in a black suit, wearing a bowler hat, and using a stick, and they replied, "Yes". That's the old man who died there. Years ago a rail track used to run across there and the old boy stepped off the train on the wrong side and was killed. But occasionally he is seen making his way across the field.

Nice little story, and the ghost was seen by more than one person.

Stories from Alex

Some people seem to attract spirits, or at least that's what they think. But actually they are more sensitive to things around them than the average person. These ghosts and spirits are there all the time; it's us that are out of sync with them. But occasionally someone like Alex comes along with the ability to see what is really there, even if he sometimes wishes he couldn't.

The first time Alex saw something that was, in his words, weird, he was a little boy and had been sent to bed by his father for being a bad lad. He was lying on the top bunk in his bedroom unable to sleep when he suddenly saw a purple light appear from nowhere. It seemed to hover in the centre of the room and within the light he could see the silhouette of three people huddled close together. The centre light was changing from purple to orange into yellow and back, continuously changing and pulsing, but the people outer ring remained the same. He remembers screaming loudly and seconds later his father burst into the room, instantly the figures vanished.

That was the first time Alex experienced something, but it wouldn't be his last. Two years later he was in the same house when without warning there was a bang from upstairs and a chandelier started to shake violently. Alex thought there must be someone else in the house, but there was nobody there but him, he was alone. The shaking stopped and all was still and quiet once more. Now you may be thinking this is the imagination of a young child and it wasn't real. However, Alex is now a grown man and about six months prior to this interview he visited a friend's house who believes that he has a spirit attached to him. On leaving that house Alex went to Stephanie's house, his girlfriend, to stay the night. Stephanie has a pet rat and Alex woke during the night and saw a dark little figure holding the cage and rocking it looking at the rat. As Alex shook his girlfriend to show her the figure it disappeared and the cage was back in its place. Two days later the same thing happened again but this time the figure was sniggering at him. He woke his girlfriend and was pointing at the figure but she could see nothing. Two days after this he was childishly playing about with his girlfriend when her jewellery box suddenly took off across the room and smashed against the opposite wall.

In one way Alex is most fortunate in being able to tune into the spirit world. Most of us will only see a ghost or experience a spirit once or twice in our lifetime. But if you were to say to Alex, he is a lucky chap, he would probably say, "Not on your life mate, you can keep them".

Recorded Voices

Sometimes it is the spirits you cannot see that make themselves known to you. EVP or, Electronic Voice Phenomena, can be recorded by most people. But if you are fortunate enough to have a spirit in your home then the EVP's can be very interesting indeed. Over the years I have heard and recorded some remarkable voices. In this particular story it is a young man by the name of Andy Harper who has successfully recorded EVP's. He regularly leaves a recorder running and is very interested in the subject. Andy lives a few miles from me and has recorded some good EVP's in his house. His father does not believe in ghosts but after hearing what Andy had recorded he said, "Andy you have to get out of that house". Recently, while Andy's baby son was staying with him his recorder picked up a woman saying "I love you". Some recordings are upbeat, some are everyday stuff, and then there are others that are a little more demonic. Andy believes, as I do, that the voices are released by the vibration of other sounds. The best example of this is to record a normal conversation in a supposed haunted location and then play it back. Other voices will be released at the same time the conversation is happening and will be on the recording when played back. It does not happen everywhere, but houses and other locations where people have experiences intense emotion seem to hold the best EVP's. Andy has researched the history of his property and knows of young deaths that have occurred there and other interesting facts. He has also left a recorder in the house when he is at work. The house is empty but he has recorded growling, and a little girl's voice calling out the name Amy. Another calls the name Lucy. In all Andy believes he has picked up nearly twelve male voices, six women's voices and three children and one dog. Now you may say, hang on a minute if the house was empty how could the voices be released? Well in my experience even white noise from electrical appliances release EVP's. All you need is noise vibration. I find Andy's interest in the voices refreshing to say the least.

Ghost Smells

You may think this is a strange title for a ghost story, but as you all know ghosts come in many forms. This story was told to me by Rachel Bignall.

Rachel lives in a red brick cottage in a small village to the west of Northampton. They moved into the property in 2002, shortly before her son was born. After only a few days there was an incident when an extremely strong smell of fish filled the cottage. They were all very fond of fish and had fish to eat regularly but on this occasion they had not eaten fish. The smell was so strong it made you retch, but strangely it vanished without trace in minutes. One day a lady came to fit some curtains and Rachel said the curtains smelt so fresh they were beautiful. Then suddenly the overpowering smell of fish filled the air once more. Again it lasted a few moments and was completely gone.

The day Rachel went into labour the smell returned, but this time it remained. Rachel's mum came to look after Rachel's daughter and asked, "Have you been eating fish pie or spilt milk or something, what's that revolting smell". Rachel told her she did not know what it was. Anyway Rachel went off to hospital but the baby was not ready to make its entrance so back she came. During that night the smell was worse than ever. Then Rachel really went into labour and was taken into hospital. Her mother back at the cottage was still suffering the bad fish smell and was convinced they had been cooking fish. When Rachel's son was finally born he was born in the cull, in the amniotic sack. The midwife was really excited as she had never delivered a baby in this way. She cut the child free and told Rachel to keep the sack as it is lucky. In olden days fishermen wore it around their neck to bring them good luck. Rachel told me they decided to keep it and dried it. Over time it disintegrated and they never thought any more about it. But after that, and to this day, the smell of fish has never returned to the house.

One night while Rachel was sitting in the living room she spotted, what she thought was one of her children running across the kitchen to the toilet. She got up, and as she did she shouted, "Why you don't use the toilet upstairs". There was no reply, and opening the toilet door there was nobody in there.

As I have explained before to people, ghosts are recordings, even a smell is part of the recording. Smell is often the last thing to remain from a deteriorating recording. At first it is full on, looking as real as you or I with sound, smell, and colour, but over time the image goes see through, the colour fades, and eventually the image disappears. That is why people report sounds and smells in their houses but rarely see anything. Rachel was lucky she saw a ghost.

Thank you for your story Rachel.

Ghost of Wootton Fields

This next story is from Carrianne. She has two children and once lived in a house at Wootton Fields in Northampton for eight months. Straight from the start Carrianne sensed a horrible feeling in the house that made her cry, she hated it. A friend visited her one day and they sat in the kitchen chatting while the children played in the garden. Carrianne got up and closed the kitchen door and her friend said, "I have just seen something". When Carrianne asked what it was her friend said she had seen a dark shape go from the window down to the side of the door. Now Carrianne had not spoken to her friend about her feelings toward the house so this came as a shock. As Carrianne was explaining to her friend that there was something strange about the house there was a loud bang upstairs as if a cupboard door had slammed. The two of them just looked at each other and Carrianne said nervously, "Let's just ignore it". Her daughter who was three at the time had a wardrobe in her room that instead of handles had cut-outs for your fingers. The door would always slam shut when you closed it. One night Carrianne heard the door slam. Thinking her daughter was up she went to investigate, but her daughter was fast asleep, why hadn't she been woken by the sound? Next morning Carrianne asked her daughter if she had heard anything during the night and her daughter shook her head. This slamming kept happening night after night, not every night, sometimes there would be a two night pause and then it would restart again. Carrianne decided to ignore it thinking it would go away.

One evening her eldest daughter was in the shower and Carrianne was bathing her youngest. On taking the youngest into the bedroom to get her ready for bed the eldest girl finished in the shower and came into the bedroom and asked her mum why she had left the tap running in the bath. Carrianne knew she had turned them off before bathing the little one. Her eldest daughter said the cold tap was open all the way. Not wanting to alarm the children Carrianne said, I must have forgotten, silly me! On another occasion Carrianne was in the living room. The stairs go up from that room. While she sat watching television she could hear muffled running about. It was not loud enough to be her children but she could still hear it.

Wanting some kind of answers Carrianne asked her sister to come over and spend time in the bedroom. Her sister is a believer in ghosts and readily agreed. She went into each of the bedrooms closed the curtains and door and started recording with a video camera. Carrianne said she would not have believed what was recorded it if she had not seen it. On the recording her sister had made, lights were flashing and streaking across the room. Her sister explained to Carrianne, this was not filmed in the girl's room, this was filmed in yours. Carrianne thought at least it's not in their room. Again she chose to ignore it thinking it would go away. Then her daughter went away with the school for a few days and on returning, that night, she screamed and came running into her mum's room. After calming her down Carrianne asked her what had happened. The girl had lain down in bed and closed her eyes. She then heard a sound, the sound made her open her eyes and as she did she saw a ball of light hovering just feet from her bed. She closed her eyes thinking it would go away, but on opening them it was still there. She reached out and turned the light on, instantly the ball disappeared so she ran to her mum. Carrianne said the girl slept in her bed for three nights and just would not go back into the room. Even now they have moved house the little girl sleeps with the light on. Carrianne told her sister about the episode and her sister said that she knew someone who could help. They arranged that the children were out of the house and the people, who were experienced in cleansing spirits from houses, came round. After a short while walking round they sat with Carrianne and explained they had discovered nine spirit names and that there was a portal within the house that allowed spirits to come and go freely, and the portal was in Carrianne's room. Unsurprisingly this didn't go down well and when they asked Carrianne if they could come back one night and contact the spirits to cleanse the house. Carrianne gave a firm answer, "No".

It amazes me even today that some experienced spiritual mediums do not take into account the way a person has reacted to a psychic event in their home. They should really stop thinking of their own abilities and self-gratification and think first and foremost about the person who has invited them into their home. Is the person ready to hear your findings and should you hold back and take things slowly and steadily. Reassurance and understanding is the key to a successful outcome for the person you are trying to help.

Carrianne has now moved house and is enjoying a normal life with her children.

Thank you Carrianne.

Ghosts of the Olde Red Lion

Now we go to the village of Kislingbury which lies to the west of Northampton to investigate the Olde Red Lion public house.

Lots of stories had filtered down the grapevine that this pub, close to where I live, was haunted. I had read that the pub had been taken over by a new landlady and was receiving excellent reviews so I phoned Ashleigh, the new landlady, to ask if I could go and talk to her about the stories I had been hearing and she kindly agreed.

The 6th of January 2014 was my first visit. I found the pub to be a very refreshing place. It was quirky, fun, and totally relaxing. Ashleigh's attitude seemed to be, if it's interesting let's give it a go. Our conversation soon centred on the reason for my visit and Ashleigh began telling me about what she, and others, had seen and heard in the short space of time they had been in the pub. In fact Ashleigh said the previous landlord had also experienced unusual activity there. The most interesting story from that period was when the landlord came down into the restaurant bar one morning to find a wine glass lying on its side in two halves. Not broken but melted, the base was still sitting on the bar upright and the top was lying on its side next to it. The glass in question was not the usual slender wine glass but a chunky old English type with a thick stem. I have never heard of this before and found the story extremely interesting. Now if I thought that was interesting, what Ashleigh was about to tell me put the previous story firmly in the shade.

Ashleigh's bedroom was directly above the pub restaurant, and during the early hours of the morning she hears rapid knocking on her door, as if someone frantically wanted her to answer the door. Each time she investigates she finds nobody there. Her ex-partner has also experienced the same thing during mid-morning, answering the door no less than three times, but again there was nobody there. Looking for obvious answers Ashleigh ruled out the door rattling because it was rapid knocking from on the outside. It still happens now but she ignores it until the knocking is accompanied with someone saying hello, then she knows it is a friend or member of staff and she will get up to answer it.

To relax Ashleigh paints pictures, and one day while painting in the back bar facing the restaurant she saw a figure walk down to the double doors on her left. She said the figure wore a black suit but you could not make out any facial features. She waited for the person to knock on the door but the knock never came. Ten minutes later it happened again, still no knock at the door. Another ten minutes went by and it happened for a third time so Ashleigh got up and went to the door, but again there was nobody to be seen. Thinking she must have imagined it she put it to the back of her mind and continued to paint. Then later in the morning Lily, who is a resident at the pub, was standing talking to Ashleigh. Lily was standing on the other side of the restaurant bar so the double doors were to her right, when suddenly she said, "What the hell was that!" She got up and went to the double doors and looked out. Ashleigh asked her what was wrong. Lily said someone dressed in black has just walked passed the doors but there is nobody there. Quickly she went out the doors on the opposite side of the room and Ashleigh went through the double doors to try to catch whoever it was, but they both ended up facing each other in the car park and saw nobody. Ashleigh then told Lily what she had seen earlier. They sat looking at each other in silent disbelief for a few seconds trying to make sense of what had happened.

Now this sighting is unusual in the fact that it happened four times in one morning and was seen by more than one person. Lily told Ashleigh exactly what she had seen; a man in a black suit with black shiny shoes and Ashleigh said she had also seen the same figure.

Over the next week or so people were talking in the pub about ghosts and so on and one of the women drinking in the bar said her step sister used to run the pub ten years previously. Apparently she came from the village and her father regularly drank in the pub. When he died he was cremated and his ashes scattered in the pub garden close to an ornamental well where flowers were then planted, foxgloves and so on. When the next people took over the pub they knew nothing of this and dismantled the well and transferred the soil to the flower borders around the upper part of the car park. When Ashleigh and Lily described to the lady in the bar what they had seen she was visibly shocked. She said from their description's they had given they had described her Dad, right down to the shiny black shoes. The woman believes the reason he is wandering the garden is because he has been disturbed from his original resting place.

Another strange thing happened in the pub's main bar only a week before my interview. Ashleigh, Christian, and two others were sat at the bar when suddenly they heard the chimes from a Westminster Clock. Then Christian saw the shadow of someone on the wall as if they were round the corner in the restaurant bar. But to replicate the shadow in the place, and the size he saw it, meant the person would have been in full view of everyone in the front bar. And there are no Westminster clocks anywhere in the building.

Ashleigh suggested I talked to Ronne Taylor, a local man who has known the pub all his life and been a regular drinker in there for over fifty years. I asked Ronne about his knowledge of the pub and he began by saying that over the years he has known many landlords come and go, and they all said there was something spooky going on in the pub. He added that they may have been told stories before moving in but he could not say for definite. I asked Ronne whether they reported activity when they were new to the pub, or when they had been in for a while. He said there wasn't really a pattern to it. He also added that in all the years he had been drinking there he had never experienced anything like ghosts and so on, but he could understand why other people may think the place is haunted. I then asked him if he was aware of the story the pub was used as a mortuary. He did remember on a wall out the back there was once a big enamel white sign that read Stretcher Depot. He also remembered a lad being killed while riding a motorbike on the bends close to the pub and they put his body temporarily in the Red Lion, but whether the pub was used as the village mortuary he couldn't say. He did explain that over the years the pub had been altered many times with bits being added on here and there. Out the back the rooms had altered radically.

Ronne then told me the story about the original Red Lion that was situated a little way up the hill on the same road. That house still stands to this day and was turned into the schoolmaster's house. Local folk law says that long ago a schoolmaster committed suicide by jumping from an upstairs window. I concluded the interview by asking Ronne whether it would surprise him if the pub was haunted, he said, "No it wouldn't".

Another local at the Red Lion is Charlotte. She has known the pub for twenty years, and even worked there for a short while. She said one day while seated at the bar something attracted her attention. It was corner of the eye stuff but enough to make her turn her head to look to her right. Through the hatchway into the restaurant she saw the figure of a man dressed in black walking up toward the doors of the kitchen situated at the far end of the restaurant. Charlotte's concentration was then broken for a split second and on looking back the figure had gone. She told Ashleigh what she had just seen and Ashleigh replied, you can't have done, we are the only people in the pub. Charlotte also noticed the figure wore a long coat because she remembered seeing the bottom of it.

The Olde Red Lion was now really intriguing me so with Ashleigh's permission I decided to do a full investigation. At 10.00pm on the 10th of February 2014 the investigation team gathered in the bar for what would prove to be a very interesting night. Our hosts for the evening were Ashleigh Fitzhugh, and Glenn Hillyard. On the investigation team were Pauline and Howard

Morgan, Lewis Dellar, Mark Thompson, and me. Pauline was our guest medium and her husband Howard was taking photos and looking after her. Mark Thompson and I were filming while Lewis Dellar was conducting interviews and would be studying people's reactions to events that would take place during the evening. As we began our walk around Ashleigh started to explain how the building had been altered over the years, she also told us a folk law tale about one previous owner who, it is believed, hid his gold up one of the chimneys. No, we didn't find it. But as you can see we had a good look

I had made a point of not telling Pauline or Howard any information that came from the interviews conducted on my previous visit. This is not intended to try to catch people out, I always make a point of doing this so any information gleaned from either the building, or from spirit, is not influenced by something someone has heard or read. Anyone who works with me knows this is how I prefer to conduct investigations. I normally allow the medium to go on a walk around first before any investigation and record their findings, but in a public house time is short and we needed to get on. We followed Ashleigh around the pub and noted anything that Pauline picked up on. At this point I thought I should just explain that although we are investigating the location, Pauline is open to spirit influence attached to the people on the investigation as well. People often forget this and get quite a surprise when a loved one suddenly gives a message through Pauline that is totally unconnected to what they thought they there for, as Ashleigh was about to find out.

The photo above shows Pauline and Howard in the pub restaurant where strange moving shadows are frequently seen by the staff. It's also a place that held a few surprises for us later in the evening.

This photo shows the point in the evening when Pauline received a message from a female spirit that wanted to tell Ashleigh she should wear her scarves more, and colour coordinate them in outfits. What none of us knew at that time was Ashleigh collected scarves and had quite a collection in her bedroom. When Pauline said it I believe Ashleigh was a little surprised.

We continued our tour of the pub and were shown to the games room. Ashleigh explained that this part of the pub was only converted about twenty / thirty years ago and was previously a garage and shed. We then walked through the bar and onto the beer cellar. Not your conventional cellar leading down steps to a damp room. Remember this pub was once a farmhouse so the pub cellar was in another room to the side of the building. Instantly on entering the cellar Pauline began to pick up the feeling of being extremely unwell. She said the person she was linking with was finding it hard to breathe and it was like they were having a heart attack. Howard confirmed this and said he was also picking up a feeling of nausea.

Through earlier investigation we knew the publican many years ago was also a butcher and it is believed the cellar was the building used for this purpose. We were then led into an adjoining room that as soon as you entered it smelt like a butchers shop.

The photo above shows Ashleigh and Pauline in the cellar.

The smell was so strong three people picked up on it. In her mind's eye Pauline could see meat hanging from hooks and people shouting. Ashleigh then drew our attention to a boarded up window with a wide windowsill. You can see it in the photo above just behind Ashleigh's shoulder. She has always thought this could have been used as a shop front to sell meat from, and looking at the room it does seem logical. The window was at the entrance to the car park so an ideal location to sell from. Pauline picked up on the names Harry or Henry attached to this room. Pauline then picked up on a female by the name of Elizabeth with two children, one boy, and a girl; Elizabeth wanted us to go up to the family rooms. Interestingly from the early 1700's William and Elizabeth Payne lived in what was then a farmhouse with their children. William combined farming with inn-keeping. He is also listed as being a butcher in 1841, until he died in 1843 leaving Elizabeth to look after their children.

As we left the cellar rooms and made our way to the restaurant I noticed Pauline getting more agitated and wringing her hands as if the energies were building. Now remember she knew nothing of the goings on in this part of the pub. Pauline started picking up on a very well dressed man who seemed very proud of the building, he also had a link to the flower foxglove, and he was looking at his watch. He seemed to be waiting for someone. Pauline then picked up on a man entering the car park on a large horse a lord of the manor type fellow wearing a bowler hat. These images faded and she picked up on the name Joseph. Pauline then picked up on someone committing suicide close to here. Now remember the story has it that a schoolmaster committed suicide by jumping from an upstairs window many years ago. Whether this is true or not I cannot say, I could find no record of this happening.

    I will give a full history of the Olde Red Lion after the main story. However, I will give some details as Pauline comes up with things I know to be true. Standing by the bar in the restaurant Pauline began picking up on a female spirit, possibly a landlady. Pauline described her as being of medium height with dark curly hair. She also wore a substantial amount of jewellery on her hands and wrists. Pauline also felt a sense of sadness while standing at the bar, and a feeling of bereavement. She then picked up on a male with the name John. She felt as though, in life, this man was pokerfaced and gave nothing away. One of William Payne's children was called John. At this point Howard, who had been standing behind the bar, signalled to me to go back further into the restaurant. He followed me and we left Pauline talking to Ashleigh. Howard said he thought he had heard the piano play and there were shuffling sounds as though someone was close to him behind the bar. I had heard nothing. Then Mark, who had been filming came over to join us and said, "You're never going to believe what I have just picked up through the microphone, the piano played, and someone was shuffling about". Howard and Mark's mouths dropped open in disbelief, they were visibly shocked, and so was I. After a few seconds to calm down we made our way back to Pauline and Ashleigh. We said nothing in case it influenced what she was getting. What she said next knocked me for six. She picked up on one or more children playing with the piano that stands by the restaurant bar and Ashleigh said people have reported hearing this being played when there is nobody in the room. How Mark, Howard, and I kept quiet I will never know, but we did.

Photo above shows Mark on the other camera. He was doing his best to stay out of shot so I swung my camera round to take this. And yes his camera footage was better than mine.

Pauline also picked up on a little boy in the main bar. She described him as having a ragged look and he wore a cloth cap and seemed to be begging, holding the cap out to people.

Pauline wanted to investigate upstairs where she felt the main lady of the house wanted her to go. So Ashleigh led us up the first flight of stairs to the pubs accommodation where Ashleigh showed Pauline her collection of scarves. The smile on Pauline's face said it all. Ashleigh then led us into the private lounge; this was a room of good proportions and one that in the past had been used as a function room for parties and so on. Pauline had difficulty picking up positive feelings in the room so Ashleigh led us along the corridor to her bedroom. I was really interested to see who Pauline would pick up in the corridor immediately outside, as well as inside the room.

Ashleigh's bedroom is immediately above the restaurant bar where the main activity seemed to be centred. Pauline felt sick as we stood immediately outside the room. Although she only said so in passing I was actually pleased. This feeling of sickness is often caused by strong spirit energy and is something you get use to in time as Pauline has done. But for Pauline to feel it in that exact spot was a good sign. I said nothing and carried on filming. On entering the room Pauline felt that children had been born there. In her mind's eye she could see a man with pull on sleeves over his forearms as if he were a doctor from way back. She could sense the manic activity surrounding a lady giving birth. Moving from there further into the bedroom we walked up into the short corridor leading to the bathroom where Pauline picked up on a large man shaving. Again she remarked that the stomach churning feeling returned. Stepping back into the bedroom Pauline said she liked this room, adding it was safe and calm, in complete contrast to the corridor outside. Ashleigh said she loved her bedroom and felt it was a refuge from the rest of the pub. She then said that the staff working and living in the pub never spend time in the old function room we had just left, and it wasn't until now that she had really thought about it, people just don't like the room. We would go back there later to find out why.

Ashleigh wanted Pauline to go further along the corridor leading off her room into the actual bathroom itself. As they did this I heard the sound of someone walking outside in the long corridor. I went out to investigate leaving Mark to continue filming, but there was nobody to be seen in the corridor. Going back into the bedroom I explained what I had just heard and Lewis decided to check it out with Howard. They both went out into the corridor and we could hear the sound of creaking floorboards again as they walked along. I asked them to come back into the room and once inside we just stood and listened.

I was trying to find out if the floorboards settled back after someone had walked over them. In some buildings this can take about a minute. People often think they are being followed as a result of boards creaking as they settle. We stood there for two to three minutes but there was no sound. So what made the boards creak while we were all in the room? Back in Ashleigh's room Pauline said that the room was where Grandma and Granddad slept. She added that this information came from a little spirit girl who was following us around with interest. We came out from Ashleigh's room I asked her to tell Pauline about the knocking on the door. After she did Pauline explained that it was the children who, way back in time, would knock and ask permission to enter a bedroom. How times have changed!

The above photo shows Pauline indicating where the little girl that was following us was standing.

I find it interesting that when we speak of the activity from spirit children it shows how children's, behaviour / etiquette, has changed. I had an incident years ago when a young person was genuinely surprised that children once asked to leave the dinner table once they had finished eating. I think the children within this household, although mischievous, knew when to use their manners. The more Pauline tells me about them the more I am convinced they come from a time the pub was a going concern rather than the farmhouse years, so we are looking at a date period after 1830 . The reason I say this is because although the children of the late nineteenth century would have been taught how to behave in public, those in the pub would have had their behaviour checked even more from constantly having so many people about.

While we stood in a bedroom the opposite side of the corridor to Ashleigh's room Pauline was drawn to a cupboard immediately behind the bedroom door. She felt a child was frantically trying to get out after being locked in during a game of hide and go seek, and the child's name was Sarah. Pauline asked where another door in the corridor led to and Ashleigh replied nowhere. Pauline felt as though there should be a way through leading to stairs. Ashleigh opened the door to what is now a cupboard but did say there were stairs there at one time but the layout had been changed.

We then made our way to the top floor of the property. This was accessed by a narrow staircase and came out into two adjoining rooms in the loft space. Pauline immediately felt the energy of an older lady with a younger woman, a maid, or someone like that who helped her.

Mark was picking up interference through his earphones linked to the camera microphone. This interference is often created my mobile phones. I asked if everyone had their phones off and the only person who had one on was Lewis. He had switched it to vibrate because he was expecting a call. But even the GPS on a phone can cause interference. Now we knew this was the case Mark could ignore it. Another interesting point is that mobile phones, Bluetooth, and other radio frequencies can give false signals on some, so called, paranormal ghost detecting equipment. I have seen someone talking to what they supposed was spirit energy coming through a 'ghost meter', when all the time it was a signal from a mobile phone that had not been switched off. Always trust your instincts and not gadgetry when investigating.

The attic space was surprisingly active with spirit energy. I suppose surprising to us as nobody had mentioned activity there before. Pauline knew the little girl was still with us and was constantly trying to understand why.

It became apparent to Lewis, Howard, and I that in one of the rooms the roof beams had been replaced. The building was not an extension so why were they relatively modern? Ashleigh had only been running the pub a short while so was still finding things out about it. Maybe in the past there had been a fire or other roof damage so the beams had to be replaced, something to look into later. Lewis also thought the pitch of the roof was too sharp, as if there was a roof beyond the one we could see. We knew the building went off to one side but there seemed to be no evidence of it up here. I left Lewis and Howard puzzling this and went into the next room where Pauline and Ashleigh were in conversation. Ashleigh's son stays up in this room and has said nothing about ghosts or whatever.

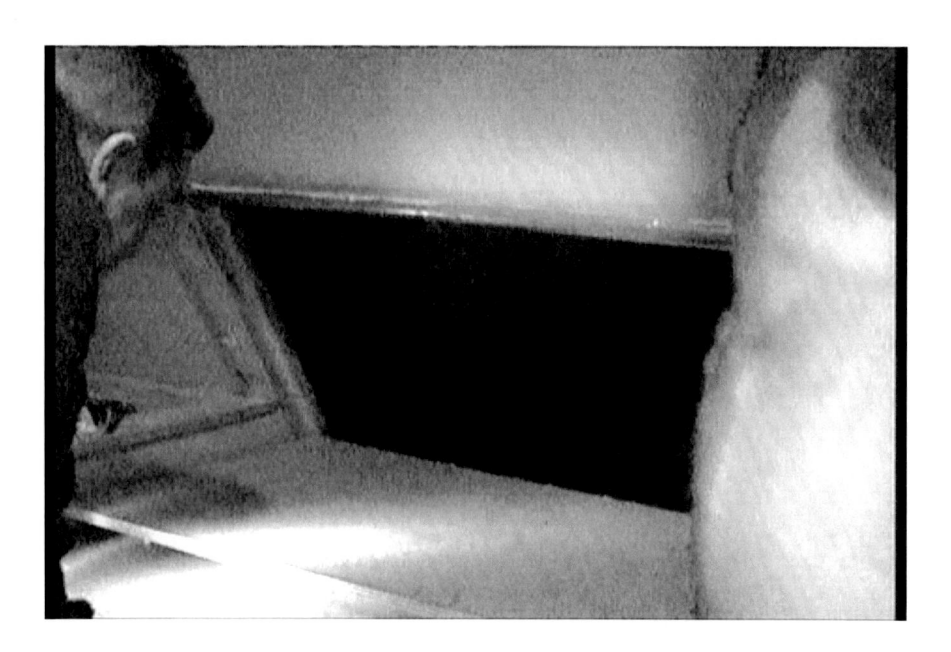

True to form Lewis was investigating in his own unique way. If there's a hidden room, or cellar, he will find it. And this time it was a hidden room he came across, as you do. A small hatchway caught his eye and quick as a flash he was peering into another room.

Without hesitation Lewis crawled into the room. It had two steps leading down so at one time it would have been accessed by a doorway. The floorboards were the old wide style and to the far end of the room was the top of a chimney stack. The pitch of the roof looked like it had been lowered and Lewis had to stoop, only able to stand in the highest point. There were bits and pieces scattered around and we all felt as though this was probably an attic space nobody could find a use for so it has been forgotten. After a good look around Lewis decided not to push his luck with the floorboards any further and came out. This attic space is directly above Ashleigh's bedroom. Little more could be gleaned from the top floor so we decided to return to the restaurant.

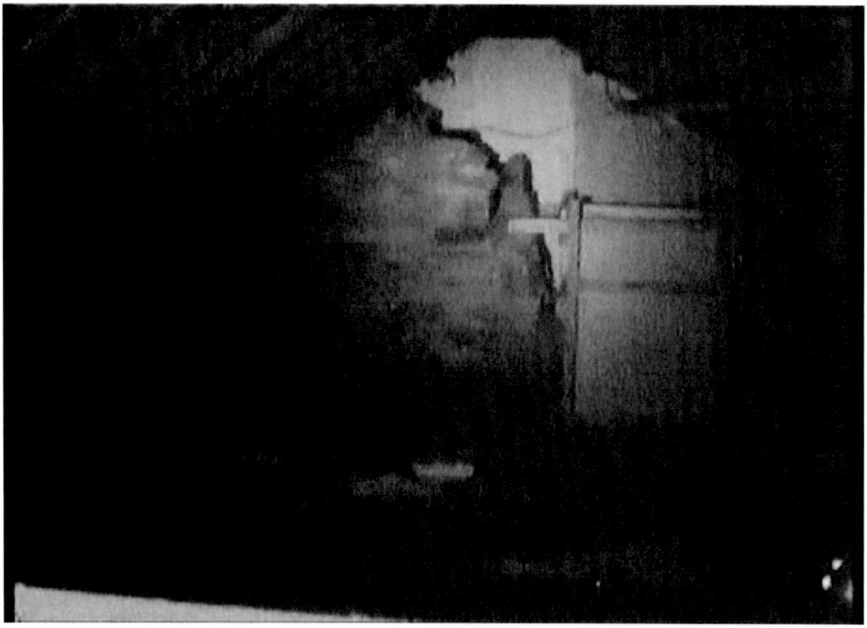

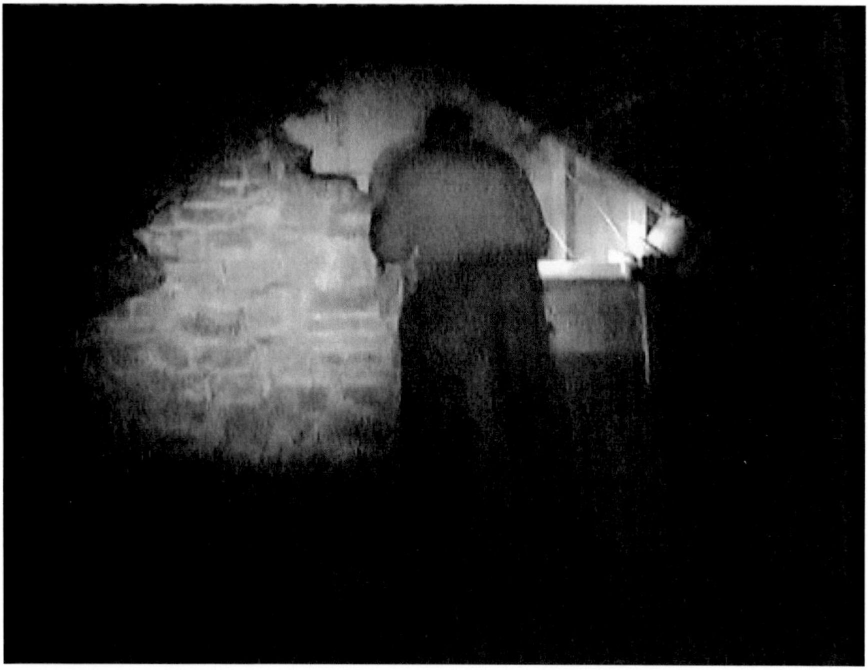

From the evidence so far it seems the most active locations within the pub were the restaurant, and the main bar. Pauline said when she first arrived in the pub she picked up on a small child in the bar. So at some point we would be conducting a séance in there. However, with the reports from the staff at the pub, and from Ashleigh herself, in conjunction with Pauline's findings, I thought the best place to do some glass divination would be in the restaurant.

A little before midnight we gathered around a table in the restaurant. We placed an upturned glass in the middle and made sure it could move without being forced. We then placed two pieces of paper on opposite sides of the table, one with yes, and one with no written on them. Seated around the table at first were Pauline, Howard, Ashleigh, and myself. Mark was filming, with Glenn and Lewis watching us, and watching for any activity around the room. You would be surprised what people miss in the way of activity simply because they are concentrating too much on the glass in front of them.

Pauline opened the circle by inviting the spirits within the building to come forward and join us. Ashleigh was a little hesitant at first so decided to sit and watch how things progressed. The rest of us reached out and placed a finger lightly on the base of the upturned glass. People were touching the glass so lightly we were barely brushing it. We first asked whether the spirit within the restaurant was male. Pauline continued asking this question for several minutes when suddenly the glass moved sharply. She repeated the question and there were slight movements, but nothing so severe. Pauline then asked if there was a female spirit in the house and the glass moved sharply again. So we now knew we had both male and female spirits here.

I then asked Lewis to ask questions to see if he provoked a response. He asked the spirits to move the glass in my direction. Instantly the glass moved, along with the table toward me. Mark was filming this and asked if we had felt what he had just seen. We looked at him and just nodded. I must admit to being a little surprised at the strength of responses we were getting. To those sceptics who say it is someone moving the glass on purpose I say this, place an upturned glass on a table and try to move the table in any direction, can't be done!

Lewis then asked the spirit to move the glass toward Pauline. Off it went, gathering speed as Pauline said come and talk to me. It then veered off and continued in a circular motion settling back right in the centre of the table. Pauline repeated the request and the glass gently glided towards her. It moved so far I could not reach it. Mark then put the camera down and joined in. Pauline then asked if the spirit was that of a little boy, no response. She then asked if the spirit was that of a little girl and the glass sped off sideways across the table toward Howard. Earlier in the evening we had heard the sound of a dog growling and Pauline asked the spirit girl if she had a dog, no movement. Then Ashleigh placed her finger on the glass and five seconds later the glass moved towards her and continued to move around that part of the table without pausing. First it went to Ashleigh, then to Pauline, and back to Ashleigh. It was becoming apparent the spirit was a little girl who obviously preferred female company. Pauline continued asking questions and the glass hardly paused between the questions. Pauline then asked three questions that got hesitant responses. The first one, "Is that you who plays on the piano?" The second, "Is that you walking along the corridor?" And the third, "Is it you knocking on Ashleigh's door?" To each question there was a pause and then a slow glide toward Ashleigh. Ashleigh then said something that had not been told to me or any of the visiting team. A little girl had been seen regularly by previous owners of the pub. Ashleigh herself has never seen her but knows of her. Strangely at that point Howard and I both felt something touch our feet. The cameras recorded nothing but there was defiantly something there.

After a short break we decided to leave the glass in the middle of the table and simply have each person seated around the table place two fingers gently on its top. Now we knew we were getting strong responses to our questions so could the spirits move the table? The table had a heavy solid wood top and an iron base. We would not be able to influence its movement in any way. But just as a precaution we had Lewis watching people and a night vision camera aimed under the table.

Interestingly Pauline thought she saw a figure go across between the restaurant and main bar but when Lewis went to investigate he could find nobody out there. As we placed our fingers onto the table I could feel a small vibration as if I were touching something attached to a machine. It was very faint and nobody else mentioned it so I said nothing. Pauline had just invited the spirits to join us when Howard and Pauline reported seeing the glass move. In fact if you look at the footage from the IR camera you can see the reflection on the glass change. Howard then said he could feel the table moving.

Lewis came in close to check it out and said the table moved to his right. I could now feel the movement, it was like someone, or something was trying to rotate the table on the spot. Lewis then got us to lift our fingers away from the table and back on again in turn. I was the last one to do it and as I put my fingers back down the table shook. Lewis had his hand on the iron framework and confirmed the movement. In fact the video footage shows more movement than we could sense. Pauline and I then placed a finger on to the glass in the centre of the table and off it went again in response to the question;

are you a child spirit? Our fingers were barely brushing the glass and it seemed to come to life as the slightest contact was made. Pauline asked whether the spirit had been a member of the Collins family and the glass shot to the word no. Did the spirit once work in the pub, again no. Then we went through a session of glass movement that never answers any questions, yes or no. It was getting frustrating beyond belief. As this continued I looked at my records searching for something I had missed. But nothing was jumping out at me, and then the glass stopped moving to any questions asked. Suddenly there was a loud thud from upstairs directly above us and when Pauline asked, was that you, the glass shot towards her. I then asked Lewis to take my place at the table to see what would happen. I had seen shadows go pass the door in the hallway and wanted to keep an eye on them. Then it happened, Pauline saw someone walk past her heading to the kitchen. I asked if it was Mary and the glass shot off again and seconds later the kitchen door opened. Lewis rushed over to see if anyone was in there messing about. He returned moments later to report that the kitchen was empty.

Photo above shows Pauline indicating where the spirit had just gone. Seconds later the kitchen door creaked as it opened. This activity seemed to be the pinnacle of the evenings activity and the rest of the session resulted in no movement whatsoever from the glass.

Let us now review the glass divination session and what our medium had sensed while walking around the pub. We know there is a little girl spirit within the pub. We also know there is a strong spirit called Mary. There is also a male spirit described as well-dressed, wearing a black suit and shiny black shoes, he also has a watch and seemed to constantly be checking the time. People have heard the sound of Westminster chimes while standing in the main bar, and someone unseen knocks on the door to Ashleigh's room.

Before we go into the last psychic session in the pub I think you should know the full history of who lived there, and when.

The Olde Red Lion first became a public house in High Street, Kislingbury when in 1829, the former Red Lion, then situated two doors away at number 17, ceased trading to become the home of the new school master. Prior to becoming the new pub the farmhouse was the home of William Payne whose family had owned and farmed here since the early 1700s. William took on The Old Red Lion licence and combined farming with inn keeping. William is also listed in the 1831 electoral register and the 1841 census as a Butcher. Family members were as follows. William, aged 40 / Elizabeth, aged 30 / William junior, aged 10 / John, aged 8 / Thomas, aged 5. Others listed in the household were Sarah Page, aged 18. When William died in 1843 records show his widow Elizabeth passed the pub license to George Hall. Then in the 1851 census Elizabeth is shown to have later married George Hall. Interestingly the children's surnames have changed from Payne to Paine. George, aged 29 / Elizabeth, aged 39 / Ann, aged 9 / Thomas aged 15. They continued as farmers, inn keepers, and butchers until the 1870s.

The Northampton brewer Pickering Phipps had by this time acquired the pub and turned it into a "tied house". The first landlord under this new system was John Harris who additionally used the premises for his butchery business. The 1881 Census states the family as follows. John, aged 26 / Elizabeth, aged 28 / John junior, aged 4 / Lilian, aged 2 / Herbert, aged 8 months. Folk law reporting a mortuary slab seen on the premises as late as the 1980's this may have been confused with a butchers slab. These old butchers' slabs had a groove running down the centre leading to a drain hole. It's strange how the macabre seems to be more appealing to people.

In 1903 Benjamin Collins, great grandfather of a recent landlord, took on the tenancy. He was a boot and shoe agent at the time but very soon began farming, continuing as publican and farmer until his retirement in 1929. His son Victor then carried on the family tradition of publican until 1947. Could the person Ashleigh and Lily saw walking by the restaurant door be Benjamin Collins the former boot and shoe agent? I think that he was one of the people Pauline Morgan picked up on by the restaurant bar. The current landlady, Ashleigh, was born locally and went to Campion School in Bugbrooke. On the following page I have put together a genealogy record of landlords and their families from 1831 to 1911. Hopefully this will help you with the concluding part of our investigation.

A history of the
Olde Red Lion 1831 to 1911

1831 Farmer, Landlord, and Butcher.　　William Payne ___ Elizabeth Payne
　　　　　　　　　　　　　　　　　　　　　　　　　　　|
　　　　　　　　　　　　　　　　　　　William　John　Thomas

1841 Farmer, Landlord, and Butcher　　William Payne ___ Elizabeth Payne
　　　　　　　　　　　　　　　　　　　　　　　　　　　|
　　　　　　　　　　　　William　John　Thomas　Ann. Ann born in 1842

1851 Landlord and Butcher　　　　　George Hall ___ Elizabeth Payne / Hall
　　　　　　　　　　　　　　　　　　　　　　　　　　　|
Children's name changed on census from Payne to Paine Ann Paine　Thomas Paine

1861 Thomas now listed as the Butcher　　George Hall ___ Elizabeth Hall
　　　　　　　　　　　　　　　　　　　　　　　　　　　|
　　　　　　　　　　　　　　　　　　　　　Ann Paine　Thomas Paine

1871 Landlord and Butcher　　　　　George Hall ___ Elizabeth Hall aged 61

1881 Landlord and Butcher　　　　　　　John Harris ___ Elizabeth Harris
　　　　　　　　　　　　　　　　　　　　　　　　　　　|
　　　　　　　　　　　　　　　　　　　　John　Herbert　Lilian

1891 Landlord and Butcher　　　　　　John Harris ___ Elizabeth Harris
　　　　　　　　　　　　　　　　　　　　　　　　　　　|
　　　　　　　　　　　　　　　　　　　　John　Herbert　Lilian

1901 Landlord, and Butcher　　　　　John Harris ___ Elizabeth Harris
　　　　　　　　　　　　　　　　　　　　　　　　　　　|
　　　　　　　　　　　　　　　　　　　　　　John　Herbert

1903　　　　　　　　　　　　　　Benjamin Collins ___ Mary Collins
　　　　　　　　　　　　　　　　　　　　　　　　　　　|
　　　　　　　　　　　　　　　　　　　　　　Edith　Victor

1911　　　　　　　　　　　　　　Benjamin Collins ___ Mary Collins
　　　　　　　　　　　　　　　　　　　　　　　　　　　|
　　　　　　　　　　　　　　　　　　　　Edith　Victor　Ida

On the eighth of January 2015 at 11.30 pm the final part of the investigation began. People attending were Ashleigh, Pauline, Howard, Glenn, Mark and his sister Abby, Lewis, and me. Because I now knew the history of the building I felt it would be wrong for me to take an active part in the glass divination and Lewis felt the same. Ashleigh had read the pub's family tree I had put together but I felt with her intimate knowledge of the pub, and being the present landlady the circle would benefit from her participation. I had drawn up pieces of paper with, male, female, boy, girl, yes, and no written on them. I needed answers to questions, but I was acutely aware I could not influence Pauline or indeed anyone else around the table by asking too many questions. All I could do is sit and check the history as information came forward. If they discover a fact I would discreetly try to glean more information without leading them.

    Pauline began as usual by inviting the spirits to join us and move the glass, if they could, in answer to questions asked. Serval minutes went by before anything happened. Then slowly the glass made very gentle movements. Pauline asked if the spirit was male or female and the glass went to female. She then asked if the spirit lived in the pub, but the glass remained at female. Serval questions later and the glass had not moved so I suggested they move the glass to the centre of the table and start again. Pauline now asked if there were any spirits of children within the pub, and if so could they channel their energy through the people present, and into the glass. It wasn't until Pauline specifically asked for a boy spirit that the glass moved to boy. Questions after that failed to move the glass. They put the glass in the middle of the table once more and I could see the frustration in people's faces. I asked Pauline to see if the spirit of Mary was here. Remember Pauline didn't know who Mary was. As they placed their fingers gently on the glass instantly it shot to yes. Pauline quickly asked if she had any children and the glass moved to yes. She asked if she had a boy or a girl and the glass moved to female. Pauline said, so you had a daughter and the glass moved to yes twice. Pauline then asked if Mary was happy, puzzlingly the glass moved to boy. I had an idea I knew what was going on. Mary Collins had two girls and one boy. I said nothing and simply asked them to continue. Several other questions came and went without movement then Ashleigh asked the question, what if the spirit could not read? Good question. But I knew what the answer to this question was going to be. Pauline asked the spirit Mary if she could read and write and the answer was, yes. Pauline went on to ask a string of questions after this but the answers made no sense at all. All the answers were boy or girl irrelevant of the question asked. Again this forms a pattern I have seen before within the pub. While filming on previous occasions it seems spirit children are playing games, cherry knocking at doors, tapping the piano keys, and opening doors, very childlike, and so we see this happening again tonight. I suggested the group change their approach so I asked Pauline to see if there were any children in the bar tonight, not necessarily living within the pub. As I asked this camera one died. On inspection it was surprisingly out of charge! I had charged three cameras before I came out so the two main cameras had thirteen hours charge and this little camera should have lasted two hours, not twenty minutes.

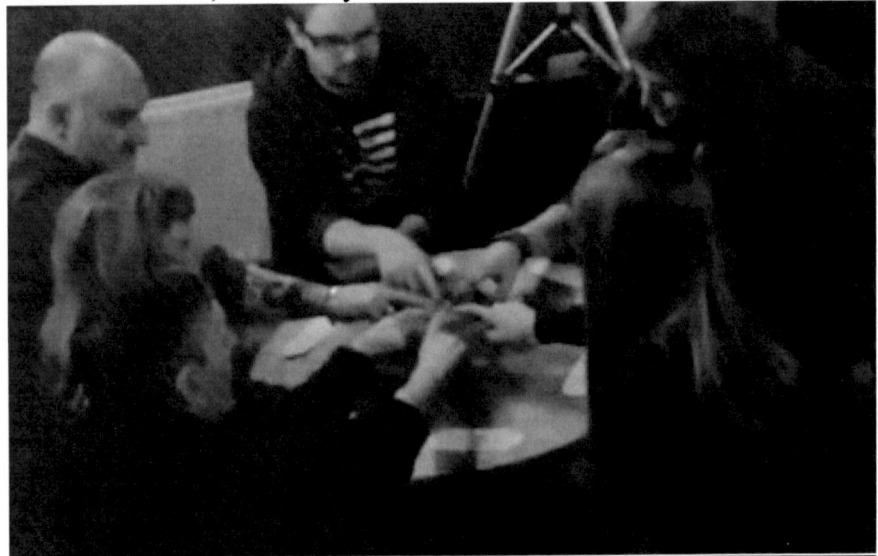

The group continued as we filmed with the remaining cameras. Pauline continued by asking if a child had switched off the camera. In response the glass moved to the word girl.

Pauline then asked, "Did the girl switch off the camera"? The glass moved to yes. Through Pauline's other questions the group managed to ascertain this was the same little girl who plays behind the bar, and on the piano. Further questions failed to move the glass so I suggested the group take a break and resume with lights out. I don't really know why this has an affect but experience has taught me that in certain circumstances it can.

Let's see what we have so far. Mary Collins, and possibly two of her three children. Names of the children would be good, but again I don't want to lead the group, so when they resume I would be asking the people within the circle to try to pick up on names in general and just shout them out, regardless how random they seem. During the break Pauline began picking up on a military man connected with the pub, she could see him dressed in army officers' uniform. There also seemed to be a woman dressed as a nurse attached to this man. She placed these two within the fourteen-eighteen war.

When we switched over to night vision and the circle reformed around the table the feeling within the pub changed instantly. I reminded people to say names as they came into their heads. I did not want to use the glass for this second session but asked the group to join hands and, led by Pauline, sit quietly and allow their thoughts to roam around the pub saying what they felt as it happened. After a quiet period of time the group began to relax. Pauline again asked about a fire connected to the pub. I could find no record of a fire damaging the pub at all. I asked them to concentrate their efforts on names connected with the building if possible. Howard picked up on the name Jack. Lewis who was operating the third Camera came up with the name Jeremiah Stone. No record could be found. Pauline then came out with Oliver and Isabel. Again no records could be found. All other names drew a blank and it was clear to me people were tired. Once fatigue sets in the nights proceedings should close.

This was not the best session we have done but it had to take place. Ashleigh and Glenn were kind enough to allow the session to take place and they were now out on their feet and extremely tired. We packed the equipment away and I thanked people for coming. As we went our separate ways I stood in the carpark with Lewis and told him it felt as though there was unfinished business to be sorted out here. He agreed, but my deadline for this book was too tight to do any more. That would be for another day and another book.

So what are my conclusions regarding The Old Red Lion in Kislingbury. Haunted? Defiantly! Do they have ghost or spirits? I believe they have both! If you were to ask me who haunts the pub I would say recent landlords, 1900's onward, and possibly their children. The only problem I have is with the children. I believe a spirit of a child has to be a child that died during childhood. From my records the children of these landlords did not. Now there's a puzzle. Or are the children from another time? Who knows!

All I can say is, visit the pub, enjoy the atmosphere and have a great time.

My thanks to Ashleigh and all at The Old Red Lion.

The Ghost of School Lane

Once again we find ourselves only a short walk from The Old Red Lion in the village of Kislingbury. School Lane, as the name suggests is a small lane running along by the school from the High-Street. This unassuming little lane was once, in the 19th century, known as Hog Lane. Again as the name suggests it was a place where pigs were kept by the tenants of cottages which once lined the lane. Only two or three cottages remain today and this story came from one of the tenants. Lisa and her family had been living in the cottage for a few years and had experienced some, as she said, "Really bizarre things happening". She had a set of battery operated tea lights that suddenly came on one night as they sat in the living room. Another time while Lisa was standing at the kitchen door a glass that had been standing on the work surface suddenly slid to one side, shot of the end smashing to the floor. Lisa explained there was no water present or draught, it simply moved of its own accord right in front of her. The family also experienced noises from upstairs. Sometimes it was the sound of someone walking across the floor and other times it was the sound of doors being opened and closed. At the time of this interview Lisa had three boys, their age range was, the youngest still a baby, middle one about six, and an older boy around eleven. The noises usually start when the baby is upstairs in his cot. As soon as a noise was heard the baby boy would squeal. Lisa said it wasn't like a baby crying for attention or because it was hungry, this was a real frightening squeal as if in pain. When she went up the little boy would be stood there sobbing. Lisa also heard sounds coming from the baby monitor. Now this in itself is not too surprising, I have tested baby monitors on other investigations and found they can pick up on taxi and normal walky-talky transmissions. But Lisa said the sounds are weird, a bit like a hoover but with moaning mixed in. When her middle boy was really small he told them a woman used to go into his bedroom. Lisa knew nothing of this at first but one of the nursery nurses looking after him asked Lisa if she had a friend staying at the house. She said she hadn't. The nurse then said the boy keeps saying an old woman keeps going into his bedroom. Lisa felt a little concerned at this news she decided to ask the boy about it. He said yes she is old and wears a black dress with a white square on it, she often comes in. Lisa thought this was just childish imagination and tried to forget it. Then one Christmas time, when the boy was about two and a half years old, he was with his mum in the living room, Lisa was watching TV *and had not noticed the boy had got up and walked from the living* room into the hallway. When she realised where he had gone it was a complete surprise to her. It must have been about ten pm and the hallway was in complete darkness. Lisa knew he was scared of the dark so for him to walk in there was strange enough, but when she walked in to find him what she saw sent a shiver down her spine. Now remember it was fairly dark in the hallway but Lisa could make out her little boy sitting on the floor pushing a toy car and saying, "Go on it's your turn". But the car never came back so the boy ran along, picked it up, returned to his spot and pushed it again saying, "Go on then". Lisa asked him who he was talking to and he replied, it's my friend mummy, it's my friend. Lisa then asked, "Where is your friend?" The boy pointed along the hallway excitedly saying, she's there mummy look she's there, it's the lady. A little freaked out by this Lisa gathered him up and took him back into the living room.

Some children do create imaginary friends, but usually they play in a place they are comfortable being in, not one that the child fears, or is uncomfortable with. Now the boy is a couple of years older he doesn't talk about the ghost. Interestingly though Lisa's father has spotted a figure in the upstairs bathroom on two occasions. Lisa went on to explain the ghost doesn't scare her anymore, in fact when she comes into the house she often says, "Evening Beryl" that's the nickname she has given the ghost. Lisa's eldest boy doesn't talk about ghosts but has said on occasion upstairs doesn't feel right. Even Lisa's mother and some of Lisa's best friends say the same thing when they walk into the house. In fact one friend won't come into the house at all it freaks her out so much.

Lisa has tried to find out about the previous owners and was told the old man who lived there actually died there. When she explained to the person who told her, she now lived in the house, the person quickly changed the story and said, well I may have made a mistake about that. Lisa told me that the majority of sounds in the property come from upstairs, and one particular evening she heard the sound of a toy at the end of her child's bed begin to play. She went upstairs to investigate and sure enough it was playing. Fortunately the child was asleep, but when she went to turn the toy off she found the switch was already in the off position. Switching it off, on, and off again stopped it. She went on to explain how she tried knocking the toy to see if that would start it, thinking her child had hit it while sleeping but the toy would not start. This has now happened more than once but Lisa now tries to ignore it. She thinks it's almost like the ghost is saying, hello I'm still here. She started to notice that doors opening and the sound of footsteps happen at about the same time in the evening, not every evening but when they do occur it's at the same time, around nine to nine thirty.

    I explained to Lisa my theory of deteriorating ghosts to help her understand a little more. My theory is this, ghost recordings deteriorate over hundreds of years. You start with an image as real as you and I with full vision, sound, and smell. You will see them, hear them walking and smell the perfume, or pipe tobacco, whatever. Slowly the image colour fades and becomes transparent. Then part of the image disappears, the head or legs remain. Then the image disappears altogether and you are left with sound and smell. The sound and smell are things people seem to experience on a regular basis. But in Lisa's case she experiences movement of objects and this is nothing to do with recordings, this is either telekinesis, (Mind over matter), or spirit based. I cannot make an informed decision about Lisa's abilities on a first visit, but her energy levels are higher than many people we have visited in the past so the possibility of telekinetic ability is there.

    Lisa had started to keep a diary of events and she showed us the previous day's entry. At nine pm the door to her youngest son's room closed of its own accord. At midnight his toy started playing at the foot of his bed. She entered the room to switch it off and again she found the switch in the off position. An even stranger thing happened a few days earlier while Lisa was sitting with her youngest son in the living room. She had decided to video him sleeping and sent the clip to her mother. As she filmed two small balls of light seem to float down into him and disappear. Lisa successfully sent the recording to her mum. But as soon as she had done this Lisa's phone stopped working and she had to get a new one. Lisa said she tried to communicate with whoever the spirit is but to no avail. She believes everything that happens in the house is done in a friendly way.

While Lisa went to make a cup of tea I discussed the activity with Lewis. I wanted his take on what he had heard. He was interested in the sounds happening at certain times during the evening and wondered if the central heating was coming on at that time and heating the floorboards making them creak? It would be logical and the heat would have that effect. Lisa came back in with the tea and said her eldest son dislikes the activity in the house and doesn't like talking about it saying it scares him a bit so they don't discuss it in front of him anymore. Going back to Lewis's theory about the central heating I asked Lisa if the activity was the same in the winter as it is during the summer and she said it was always the same. Lisa suggested we go upstairs so she could show us the layout and explain things better. At the top of the stairs a fairly long landing leads off to the bedrooms and bathroom. At one end is the master bedroom. Even without Lisa saying you could feel the difference as you crossed the threshold into that room. When I say difference that's what it is. It's, a difference in feeling, almost like an invisible barrier you walk into. This feeling is not present in the newer extension. The upstairs seems significantly different to the downstairs and if you were to ask me where the activity in the house was strongest I would point upstairs. After a good look around we discussed with Lisa what, if anything, she wanted to do next. Because she was happy with the ghost being there she did not feel anything needed to be done. Lewis and I agreed, but did ask Lisa to continue keeping the diary and I told her to contact me at any time should things happen that were unusually different. She agreed and we left it at that. A few weeks later Lisa phoned me to tell me about a most bizarre thing that had just happened. She had a friend round for a catch up and they suddenly heard this strange knocking noise. On investigation they found Lisa's phone that was upstairs had bounced its way to the bottom of the staircase. It wasn't broken in any way, but how did it move off the side table to actually bounce down the staircase, when there was nobody else in the house?

I was unable to get to Lisa's house for a few weeks and by the time I could they had decided to move to a new home. Not because of the ghost but because they were building a new home and it had been completed. So will we ever know who the ghost was, I have done some digging in the archives, and although I cannot divulge the name in this book, Lisa's idea about a previous tenant was right. He probably enjoyed the company of children and the energy they had.

Thank you Lisa.

Braunston Tunnel

My wife Denise and I were having dinner one evening with our good friends, Tim Casentieri and his wife Roberta, both have a wealth of knowledge regarding boating life on rivers and canals having lived on a boat for many years. Tim began telling me about Braunston Tunnel, they frequently navigate through it as they travel along the Grand Union Canal. The tunnel has an interesting history and Tim also suspects it may be haunted due to their experiences while there. He knew I could not resist a good story, and knew I would jump at the chance of a trip through the tunnel, but he would not elaborate on his experiences. I needed no further persuasion and, with their permission, we set a date to go in and see what we could find.

This is what I know about the tunnel. It is situated on the Grand Union Canal about 830 yards east of Braunston Northamptonshire and is 2,042 yards in length. Built by Jessop and Barnes, the tunnel is 4.8m wide by 3.76m in height. It was opened in 1796 but its construction was delayed by soil movement and it was probably this movement that lead to the tunnel having a slight 'S' bend in its length. The tunnel passes underground alongside another Grand Union Canal feature, Drayton Reservoir from which the feeder enters the canal at the east end of the tunnel.

Now I had to decide who to call on for assistance to make this investigation work. Lewis Dellar, definitely as he will look for the logical answers. Now for a medium, Pauline Morgan has been on many recent cases and has an excellent reputation for being accurate in her findings. Howard Morgan, Pauline's husband, is a dab hand at photographing the unusual and can turn his hand to most things. After contacting these three and chatting to Tim and Roberta we were good to go. On Saturday the 14th of September 2013 we met at Braunston Marina. Tim gave us a safety chat should anything go wrong during the tunnel run. As Pauline, Howard, and Lewis had never met Tim and Roberta I thought it a good idea to get there a little earlier so we could all get acquainted. As with all likeminded people it didn't take long for friendships to start and the laughter soon began. Having fun on investigations is a must, and with Tim and Roberta as our hosts it was guaranteed. Here is a little advice from me. When doing an investigation make it a sociable event and have a laugh. Many investigations are done in a way that is too serious and clinical. This in turn leaves people feeling let down and not wanting to do one again, so get stuck in and have some fun.

From the left, Lewis, Pauline, Howard, Tim, and Robert.

During the run through the tunnel Pauline, Howard and Roberta would be up front inside the boat, Howard recording Pauline's findings. Tim, Lewis, and I would be by the tiller and possibly getting extremely wet as most canal tunnels have rainwater cascading down at the various air shafts dotted along their length. However, the company more than made up for what the tunnel may throw at us. As we drifted slowly towards the tunnel entrance I could hear faint talking coming from the front of the boat. Was Pauline already picking someone up? I had a feeling this journey was going to be a little different to our normal investigation routine.

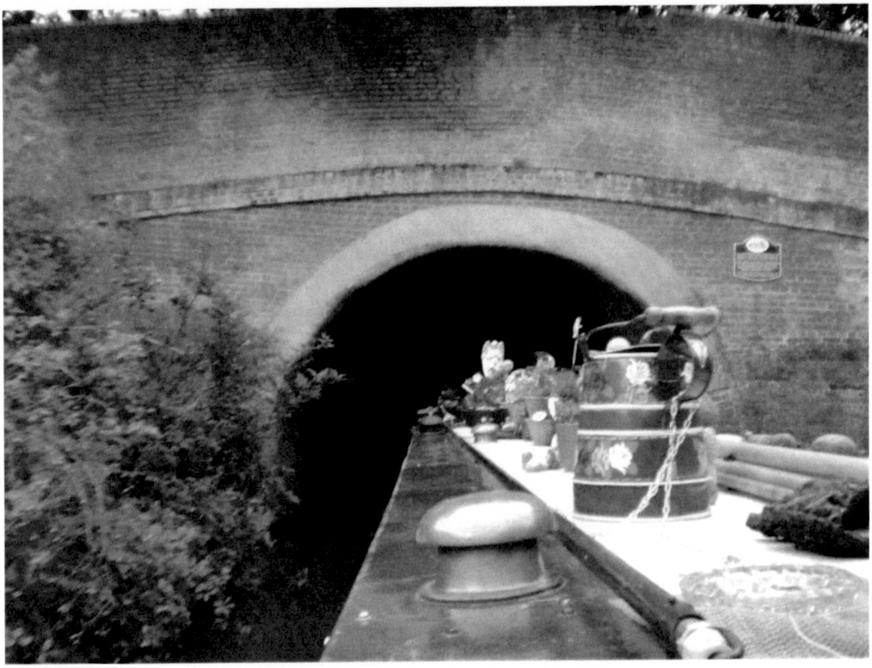

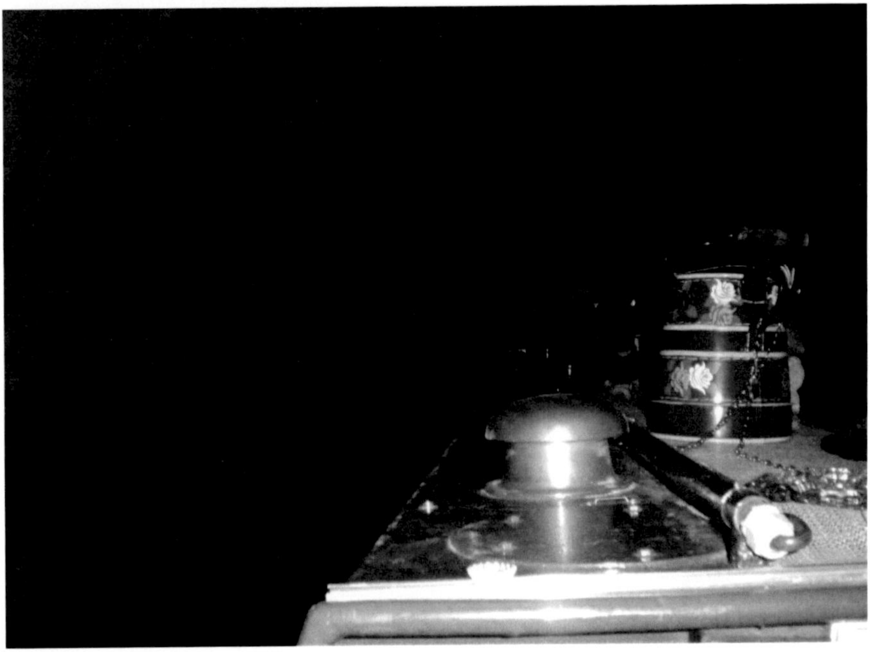

Once inside the tunnel, looking back the daylight fades all too quickly.
The lights from the boat illuminated the tunnel creating an eerie claustrophobic atmosphere that was hard to ignore.

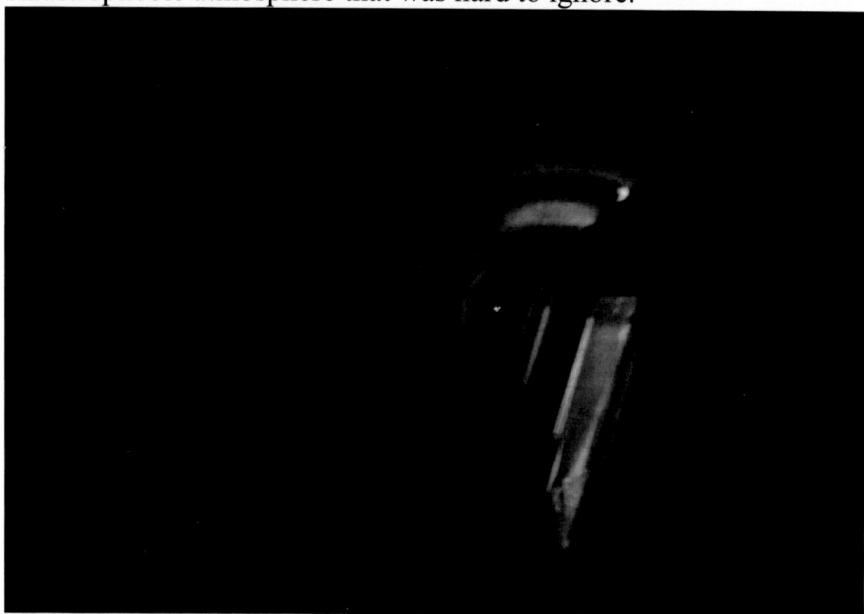

We now focus our attention to the front of the boat where Howard had started to record what Pauline was sensing.

Pauline first picked up on a man travelling into the tunnel and suffering badly with heart pains. Pauline was getting disorientated and finding it difficult to judge distance and feels the man suffered a major heart attack close to the centre of the tunnel and his boat continued through after he had died. Tim shut the throttle down on the engine and allowed the boat to drift for a minute to allow Pauline a real sense of solitude. She started picking up on one of the engineers and sensed the original plans of the tunnel had not been followed and they had been altered to what we see today. It had something to do with the ground surfaces not being reinforced and subsequent movement to part of the tunnel. Pauline then sensed a Scottish man called Harry who transported goods for the cotton industry, but he usually travelled a London, Birmingham route. As we travelled deeper into the tunnel Pauline started to get a real strong sense of a woman who had given birth while travelling through. It was in the days when boats were legged through and this happened to the woman, not once, but twice. Both her sons had been born while in the tunnel and both went on to work on boats as many generations of families had done. Pauline felt as though the boating people she was picking up on had a closed community that seemed to fend for itself, both in medical, and in times of trouble. Non boating people were outsiders and should be treated as such.

Pauline was right in what she was sensing. Many people viewed boating families as water gypsies and of no importance. They were not to be trusted and were looked down upon by many. Same old story really, fear and mistrust someone or something you don't understand. In fact the boating fraternity were hard working people just trying to earn a living from the transportation of goods. Their way of life was hard but the sense of community was extremely strong and effective. It was the building of the railways that rang the death bell for their way of life. Strange how we now crave the solitude of a life on water. Pauline was getting so much information it was really hard for her to get a consistent contact and a whole story without interruption.

As we drifted towards the exit of the tunnel Pauline said she felt a sense of calm and peace that was quite remarkable after the turmoil of emotions the journey had delivered, but she felt as though the spirits wanted her to go back as they had more to reveal. As we emerged and travelled alongside the towpath she sensed children running alongside as if to greet us at the end of our journey.

As we stepped from the boat Lewis came up with two names, James Bonham and Patricia Rawlinson. Both names need further investigation.

Now it's time to reflect on our trip through what is a relatively short tunnel.

Surprisingly we stayed dry up by the tiller and had a pleasant ride through. We chatted about the history and the tunnels construction and left Pauline to contact the spirits. It's not surprising Pauline found it confusing, with so many energies that have travelled through the tunnel trying to pick just one or two was always going to be difficult. Saying that I think the information she did pick up on has given me a starting point on future research. Now I wanted to know what Tim and Roberta had experienced on their many journeys through. Tim said that on several occasions he had heard a boat behind him and saw its light following, but on tying up at the towpath after exiting the tunnel the boat never emerged. They both

said they have sensed people with them during the run through Braunston.
So is the tunnel haunted? Well why don't you try it and find out for yourself.

Let me know how you get on!

Ghost of Yellow Cottage

In the village of Weedon Bec, west of Northampton stands a quaint little cottage known as, Yellow Cottage. The owners are Renee and Alex. They began their story by explaining a little of their history. Their cottage was nearly two hundred years old, and at the time of this interview they had lived in it for twenty seven years. Renee went on to explain that they had what she described as, a presence within the house, specifically in the main bedroom. On numerous occasions over the years she gets tucked into bed as if she were a child being tucked in by her parents. The unseen figure then sits on the bed, forming a depression. Renee and Alex had never discussed this with friends or family preferring to keep it quiet. However, some friends of theirs living in Monte Carlo came over to stay with them for a few days. At breakfast one morning the friend said, somebody tucked me in last night; the duvet was tucked right under me quite tightly. The other interesting point to note about this story is this strange phenomenon only occurs in Renee's side of the bed and never on her husband's side. Renee also has a small balcony on her side of the bedroom and on certain occasions she gets a strange smell drifting in from outside or at least that's what was first thought. She found it hard to describe the smell; it's like the burning smell of metal that is so strong it actually hurts her nostrils making her eyes water, but her husband Alex never smells it. Renee has had two psychics visit the house on separate occasions and without prompting they described a burning smell. I asked Renee whether there was a forge close by. Well, many years ago an army barracks, still standing today, was fully occupied and they also housed a good number of horses along with all the paraphernalia that goes with the looking after them. Could this be a memory from the past that is captured on the wind? Well here is the puzzling thing; the house has secondary glazing and the other night all the windows and doors were shut so the house was sealed tight, but the smell was as strong as ever. Renee and Alex have now come to the conclusion that the smell is generated from within the property and can last over an hour. We do know the house next door caught fire and was badly damaged some forty years ago.

Alex then went on to describe another phenomena that they have experienced when entering the house through the front door. He described how there was a distinct temperature drop that coincided with a strong smell of fish. He said this can happen at any time of the year and it lasts for a few seconds then completely vanishes.

Renee has the deeds to the cottage going back to when it was first sold and many of the first tenants were farm workers employed by the local estate, but there was little that could explain the events within the house. One of the visiting mediums was quite badly affected by what they discovered. Renee when on to explained what they sensed happened. The door to the balcony was not original and long ago it was a simple window about three feet from the floor. In front of this window stood a small piece of furniture; a little girl living in the house climbed onto the furniture and leant out of the window tragically falling to her death. The grieving mother of the child is said to tuck you in tightly as she would have done her little girl, only now it's a penance carried out through guilt for not being able to save her child. I was keen to understand the mediums thoughts so I asked Renee if Lewis and I could go up to look at the room, she agreed and led the way. On entering the bedroom you could feel a difference in atmosphere it was tangible. Even logical Lewis came up with a name as we stood by the balcony door, Terrance Morgan. Renee recognised the name from the deeds and said, "You're right, I think there is a Morgan in the deeds". I think Lewis was more surprised than anyone, but he has been very accurate in the past, not bad for a logical psychologist! My own feelings concurred with that of the medium who visited earlier, a small child and a grieving woman. However the story told to me earlier may have led my thoughts so I have to discount my personal findings.

Renee and Alex are completely happy in their home and I can't say I blame them, it is a lovely cottage. Back downstairs Alex wanted to show us something. He led us back through the living room and into the kitchen. Apparently this cottage was once two smaller cottages and the kitchen is where the other cottage started. Recently, well within living memory; this second cottage was used as a shop with a narrow alleyway separating them. The story is that a cow escaped from the local abattoir and ran down this alleyway and promptly got stuck. The farmer rescued the cow which instead of being returned to the abattoir was led to one of his fields and released, reprieved for a few days at least. In the cottage deeds the alleyway was designated as a pathway used by villagers to collect water from a deep well in the back garden. The owners of this cottage charged tuppence for each pail of water drawn from the well.

All properties go through structural changes throughout their lives and these cottages were no exception, being knocked into one larger dwelling. It's a sign of the times and how our living tastes have changed. But we need to remember that recordings of people from the past have their images set into the very atmosphere around us. Nothing we do will alter the path they walk. I don't mean that in a spiritual way but in a physical one. Build walls, knock down stairs, or block doorways, the recording will always follow its original route. It is a spirit within this house, not a ghost. The latter cannot physically interfere with our surroundings, only a spirit can do this. Remember what Renee said, you can see a depression in the bed as it sits down! A recording, or ghost, doesn't open doors or move objects, it can't; only spirit energy can do this. This story is one that needs following up and investigating further. Unfortunately at the time of writing this book we are unable to go forward with this. However, I thought it would be a story you would like to read and would certainly give you food for thought. Hopefully I will be able to give you more information in the next book.

From the Author

It seems a very long time ago when I first set out to bring you new stories of ghostly goings on. Techniques' and ideas have changed very little in this time and it constantly frustrates me to see this. I know I have said in the past I love to see people looking for spirits in their own way, but time and time again they use the same old ways. I would like all paranormal groups and individuals to push further. Look at what others have done and try to change your approach. I am as guilty as anyone of following the trend. However, I have tried to bring psychology and logical reasoning into the investigations in an attempt to see beyond the obvious beliefs and mind-sets people have. In future investigations I will be leaving gadgetry behind and focusing on the human mind and its abilities to affect its surroundings.

Many people who start out as paranormal investigators end up going down the commercial route because they feel they have done what they can and there is no more they can do. They run ghost tours, ghost nights and so on. To these people I say this, if you are really determined to find answers to the questions you had when you first started out, then put your gadgets away and start studying the human mind. It's the power of the brain and the mysteries of our unknown abilities that hold the key to future development of paranormal investigation, not gadgets, just people.

Until next time.